Alejandro García-Cintado · Diego Romero-Ávila
Carlos Usabiaga

Spanish Regional Unemployment

Disentangling the Sources of Hysteresis

Springer

Alejandro García-Cintado
Diego Romero-Ávila
Carlos Usabiaga
Pablo de Olavide University
Seville
Spain

ISSN 2191-5504 ISSN 2191-5512 (electronic)
ISBN 978-3-319-03685-4 ISBN 978-3-319-03686-1 (eBook)
DOI 10.1007/978-3-319-03686-1
Springer Cham Heidelberg New York Dordrecht London

Library of Congress Control Number: 2013957709

Printed on acid-free paper

Springer is part of Springer Science+Business Media (www.springer.com)

SpringerBriefs in Economics

For further volumes:
http://www.springer.com/series/8876

Acknowledgments

We thank Jesús Crespo-Cuaresma, Miguel León-Ledesma, Daniel Oto-Peralías and Simon Wren-Lewis for valuable comments and suggestions. The authors acknowledge financial support from the Spanish Ministry of Science and Technology through grant ECO2009-13357, the Spanish Ministry of Economics and Competitiveness through grant ECO2012-35430 and the Andalusian Council of Innovation and Science under Excellence Project SEJ-4546.

Contents

Abstract

This work investigates the time series properties of the unemployment rate of the Spanish regions over the period 1976–2011. For that purpose, we employ the PANIC procedures of Bai and Ng (2004) which allow us to decompose the observed unemployment rate series into common factor and idiosyncratic components. This enables us to identify the exact source behind the hysteretic behaviour found in Spanish regional unemployment. Overall, our analysis with three different proxies for the excess of labour supply renders strong support for the hysteresis hypothesis, which appears to be caused by a common stochastic trend driving all the regional unemployment series. In the second part of the analysis, we try to determine the macroeconomic and institutional factors that are able to explain the time series evolution of the common factor, and in turn help us shed light on the ultimate sources of hysteresis. We shall see how the variables that our empirical analysis emphasises as relevant closely fit into the main causes of the Spanish unemployment behaviour. Finally, some policy considerations drawn from our results are presented.

Keywords Unemployment rate · Persistence · Productivity · PANIC · Common factor · Spanish labour market

Chapter 1
Introduction

Abstract Over the last decades, the Spanish economy has stood out as the advanced country with the highest unemployment rate. This outrageous figure has encouraged many international researchers to embark on the study of this phenomenon from different perspectives, with the hope of coming up with an adequate solution. In addition to being exceptionally high, the Spanish rate of unemployment has also turned out to be abnormally persistent, as many econometric studies have highlighted. Empirical work using unit root and stationarity tests has tried to discriminate among alternative macroeconomic schools/paradigms as regards the distinct approach to the labour market. In the case of the Spanish unemployment rate, the majority of such work overall points to a highly hysteretic scenario.

Keywords Unemployment rate · Spanish labour market · Hysteresis

Over the last decades, the Spanish economy has stood out as the advanced country with the highest unemployment rate. Actually, in the second quarter of 2013, the unemployment rate made available by the Spanish Labour Force Survey (EPA) reached the astonishing number of 26.2 %, becoming even 10 % points higher in regions like Andalusia (Usabiaga 2004). Moreover, according to the so-called Okun's law (Usabiaga 2010), the dismal economic growth figures forecast for 2014 by both national and international analysts anticipate that no meaningful unemployment reduction will occur shortly –see García-Cintado and Usabiaga (2013). Thus, although it is a problem that dates back some decades –see Blanchard and Jimeno (1995)–, it still remains a highly topical subject, having become even more important in recent times.

This outrageous figure, both in absolute and relative terms, even within a neighbourhood of countries whose unemployment rates are worrisome (Blanchard 2006), has encouraged many international researchers to embark on the study of this phenomenon from different perspectives, with the hope of coming up with an adequate solution. In addition to being exceptionally high, the Spanish rate of unemployment has also turned out to be abnormally persistent, as many econometric studies have highlighted. In fact, previous works have made an attempt to explicitly discriminate among alternative macroeconomic schools/paradigms as

A. García-Cintado et al., *Spanish Regional Unemployment*, SpringerBriefs in Economics,
DOI: 10.1007/978-3-319-03686-1_1,

regards the distinct approach to the labour market. More specifically, on the one hand, there is the traditional natural rate theory, pioneered by the work of Friedman (1968) and Phelps (1967, 1968), that holds the view that the unemployment rate tends to fluctuate around some equilibrium level associated with a fully equilibrated labour market where all adjustments have worked themselves out. This natural rate hypothesis can be featured with a stationary autoregressive process in which the variable reverts back to its mean at a rapid pace. It should be noted that this mean is not independent from the structural characteristics of each economy, but rather it does hinge on them. On the other hand, the structuralist hypothesis – Phelps (1994) and Phelps and Zoega (1998)– delves into the same line of argument and indeed upholds that a natural rate of unemployment exists, toward which the actual rate tends to revert back, but it differs from the former hypothesis in that the natural rate may be subject to infrequent changes as a result of the occurrence of shocks to fundamental variables of the economy, some of which can be internationally determined—energy prices, real interest rates, real exchange rates, technological factors, etc. Only if the unemployment rate showed a behaviour compatible with that of an I(0) time series, once structural breaks had been accounted for in the analysis, would it be safe to assert that the structuralist hypothesis held. Finally, even if after controlling for structural breaks, this behaviour resembled more that of an I(1) process, an extreme form of persistence (or "hysteresis"[1]) would be expected to prevail –Blanchard and Summers (1986, 1987)–, thereby rendering the mean-reverting process non-existent, which in practical terms means that any potential shock would have a permanent effect on the economy. Think of, say, contractionary macroeconomic policies as having long-lasting effects on the unemployment rate. Although it might sound somewhat striking to those unfamiliar with the literature, many macroeconomists and labour economists see this otherwise unlikely scenario –that of complete hysteresis– as entirely suitable for the case of the Spanish economy.

From a unit-root tests perspective, this literature, which has strived to account for those aforesaid theoretical frameworks, has basically evolved in the following way: (i) Individual time series without breaks; (ii) Individual time series with breaks; (iii) Panel data without breaks; (iv) Panel data with breaks. In some cases, instead of unit root tests –which are mainly linear–, stationarity tests are employed. The latter involve switching the null hypothesis. As panel data techniques have become more fashionable, special heed has been paid to the cross-sectional dependence across series. It is worth noting that the analysis of the Spanish rate of unemployment has been approached from all these distinct perspectives,[2] in

[1] Digging deeper into the terminology, the (full) hysteresis case implies that every temporary shock affects unemployment permanently, thus making the traditional concept of natural rate irrelevant (Karanassou and Snower 1997). On the other hand, the partial hysteresis or persistence case entails that temporary shocks have long-lasting but not permanent effects. The hysteresis case can be modelled as a unit root process while the persistence one as a near unit root.

[2] There are some alternative econometric approaches which could also be employed to measure persistence: fractional integration, estimation of half-lives in the presence of a disturbance, etc.

isolation from or in conjunction with other economies (at the European level, OECD, etc.), and even in certain cases, have some studies been undertaken at the regional level. As already mentioned above, in the case of the Spanish unemployment rate, the majority of such work overall points to a highly hysteretic scenario. In addition, it may be interesting to stress that European unemployment rates are found to be more persistent than the U.S. one—see as a sample Romero-Ávila and Usabiaga (2007, 2008, 2009).[3]

At this stage, from an industrialised country perspective, a question that immediately comes to mind is how the Spanish unemployment rate can be so high and persistent. One of the traditional explanations goes as follows: Spain –and other European countries– suffers from "Eurosclerosis" –see Layard et al. (1991) and Nickell et al. (2005)–; that is, Spain could be regarded as an extreme case within Europe as far as the existence of rigidities in the goods and labour markets is concerned (firing costs, unemployment insurance, taxes, barriers to free market, etc.). As is well known, Blanchard and Wolfers (2000), working on a panel of OECD countries, enhanced this line of argument by focusing on the interactions of shocks and unemployment-prone institutions as the correct way to account for the high and persistent European unemployment.

As for the high persistence, the long-term unemployment trap approach[4] (discouragement effect, loss of specific skills, stigma effect, etc.) and, especially, the insider–outsider models –Blanchard and Summers (1986, 1987), and Lindbeck and Snower (1988)– can be thought of as the two most widely used explanations for the Spanish case. It is no surprise that the main Structural Vector Autoregression (SVAR) analyses carried out for the Spanish economy, which comprise the variable unemployment, have relied on the insider–outsider framework under complete hysteresis (Gómez and Usabiaga 2001). The focus on long-term unemployment as a plausible account of the Spanish unemployment problem only makes sense primarily up to 1992–1993, when a profound reform of the unemployment insurance system was enacted, leading the country to go unnoticed when compared to other European countries concerning the generosity of those benefits. On the other hand, the "insider–outsider" interpretation closely relates to the dual or segmented labour market approach, and it arises as a powerful potential reason for explaining the notoriously high share of fixed-term labour contracts[5] and its

[3] Romero-Ávila and Usabiaga (2007) make use of a panel unit root test (Lee and Strazicich 2003) and Romero-Ávila and Usabiaga (2008, 2009) employ a panel stationarity test (Carrión-i-Silvestre et al. 2005), allowing for up to two and five level shifts, respectively.

[4] The long-term unemployment problem has virulently returned as a result of the current economic crisis. Thus, throughout the second quarter of 2013, around 60 % of the unemployed were out of work for more than 12 months.

[5] Due to the 1984 labour reform, which gave birth to a regularly used non-causal fixed-term contract with low severance pay, the Spanish temporary employment rate climbed from roughly 12 % to a number that has been hovering around 30–35 % since 1990, thereby doubling the European Union average. This number has declined approximately 10 % points during the current crisis owing to the intense destruction of temporary employment. On the problem of excessive temporary employment predicament in Spain, see for example Dolado et al. (2002).

side effects (excessive rotation, low productivity, low company-based education, job-related accidents, etc.). It is therefore no wonder that this model has lived on as a satisfactory accounting of the Spanish labour market behaviour (Bentolila et al. 2012a, b, c).

In fact, the unsuccessful attempts of reforming the Spanish labour market (1984, 1994, 1997, 2001, 2002, 2006) –see Usabiaga (2007)–, have ended up giving rise to a widespread and lively debate on the effects of the last labour reforms in the wake of the Great Recession (2010, 2011, 2012), and especially on the proposal of the "single open-ended labour contract", whose foremost feature turns out to be the increasing –with tenure– severance pay for all new hiring. According to its advocates, it aims at tackling the insider–outsider predicament, by doing away the existing severance pay gap between permanent and temporary labour contracts.[6] Other theories that might succeed in accounting for the dynamics and persistence of the Spanish regional unemployment are the Chain Reaction Theory (Karanassou and Snower 1997, 1998), whereby movements in unemployment can be viewed as the outcome of the interplay between macroeconomic shocks and a network of lagged adjustment processes; the theories that rest on adjustments through labour participation versus those brought about via migration –Blanchard and Katz (1992), Decressin and Fatás (1995)–; and finally those approaches relying more on wage behaviour (Blanchflower and Oswald 1994).

In this work, we intend to shed some new light on the high and persistent Spanish unemployment rate –a variable that sparks a great deal of attention among international observers– by employing a novel econometric methodology that allows for strong forms of cross-sectional dependence. This methodology has proven to be very useful in other fields and we think it really fits the nature of the issue at hand, leading to a new analytical perspective. Given that it is a panel data technique, we shall work with series of the Spanish regions, mainly focusing on the data provided by EPA. We should underline that we also apply the same methodology to two other indicators of excess labour supply stemming from the National Public Service of Employment (Servicio Público de Empleo Estatal, SPEE) –the former National Institute of Employment (Instituto Nacional de Empleo, INEM)–, without significant changes in the main conclusions, which leads us to think of our results as highly robust.

More specifically, this work employs the Panel Analysis of Nonstationarity in Idiosyncratic and Common components (PANIC) framework developed by Bai and Ng (2004). Unlike most tests employed in this field, the PANIC approach allows for strong forms of cross-sectional correlation such as cross-cointegration. Previous studies have emphasised the fact that failure to allow for cross-dependence when it is present in the data can cause severe size distortions (see O'Connell 1998; Maddala and Wu 1999; Banerjee et al. 2005). PANIC methods

[6] As a proposal based on search and matching models endorsing the use of the single open-ended contract, see Costain et al. (2010) and García-Pérez and Osuna (2012). In these papers, the authors contend that such a type of contract induces better dynamics in the labour market than the dual employment protection legislation.

will enable us to (i) investigate whether there is cross-sectional dependence driven by one or several common factors and (ii) determine whether the source of nonstationarity is the common factors or the idiosyncratic components. In this work, we thus extend the analysis of the time series properties of Spanish unemployment at the regional level by employing these PANIC techniques. The high and persistent level of Spanish unemployment which has sustained over the past three and a half decades is considered to be one of the most striking cases for the hysteresis hypothesis. Determining which components of the observed unemployment rate series are driving the high persistence in the series is necessary if one wants to formulate economic policy prescriptions in order to tackle the unemployment problem over the medium term. Overall, our empirical analysis renders overwhelming evidence of nonstationarity in the regional unemployment rate series, which appears to be driven by a common stochastic factor. In the event of stationary idiosyncratic series, the evidence supports the existence of pairwise cointegration across regional unemployment rate series. In practical terms, these results indicate that the hysteretic behaviour in Spanish unemployment observed across all regions is caused by a common force that appears to exhibit nonstationarity. Remarkably, the results are robust to the use of three different proxies for the excess of labour supply.

The second part of the study tries to identify which factors (macroeconomic, labour, institutional, etc.) are able to characterise the common stochastic trend driving Spanish regional unemployment rates. Towards this end, we will employ Granger-causality testing based on VAR analysis with variables entering the system in stationary form. By determining the factors responsible for such common hysteretic patterns in Spanish unemployment, we will be in a position to suggest policies that can help tackle this problem.

The remainder of this study is structured as follows. Chapter 2 describes the unemployment data, the PANIC econometric methodology, and the results from the decomposition of the observed unemployment rate series of the Spanish regions into a common and an idiosyncratic component and their respective time series properties obtained via PANIC. Chapter 3 tries to determine the economic and/or institutional variables able to explain the common stochastic trend present in Spanish regional unemployment. Chapter 4 draws policy lessons from our overall empirical results. Finally, Chap. 5 concludes.

References

Bai J, Ng S (2004) A PANIC attack on unit roots and cointegration. Econometrica 72(4):1127–1177

Banerjee A, Marcellino M, Osbat C (2005) Testing for PPP: should we use panel methods? Empir Econ 30(1):77–91

Bentolila S, Cahuc P, Dolado JJ, Le Barbanchon T (2012a) Two-tier labour markets in the great recession: France versus Spain. Econ J 122(562):F155–F187

Bentolila S, Dolado JJ, Jimeno JF (2012b) The "new" new labour market reform in Spain: objectives, instruments, and shortcomings. CESifo DICE Rep 10(2):3–7

Bentolila S, Dolado JJ, Jimeno JF (2012c) Reforming an insider-outsider labor market: the Spanish experience. IZA J Eur Labor Stud 1(4):1–29
Blanchard OJ (2006) European unemployment: the evolution of facts and ideas. Econ Policy 21(45):5–59
Blanchard OJ, Jimeno JF (eds) (1995) Unemployment in Spain: is there a solution? Centre for Economic Policy Research (CEPR), London
Blanchard OJ, Katz L (1992) Regional evolutions. Brookings Pap Econ Act 23(1):1–76
Blanchard OJ, Summers LH (1986) Hysteresis and the European unemployment problem. NBER Macroecon Annu 1:15–78
Blanchard OJ, Summers LH (1987) Hysteresis in unemployment. Eur Econ Rev 31(1–2):288–295
Blanchard OJ, Wolfers J (2000) The role of shocks and institutions in the rise of European unemployment: the aggregate evidence. Econ J 110(462):1–33
Blanchflower D, Oswald A (1994) The wage curve. MIT Press, Cambridge
Carrión-i-Silvestre JL, Del Barrio T, López-Bazo E (2005) Breaking the panels: an application to the GDP per capita. Econometrics J 8(2):159–175
Costain J, Jimeno JF, Thomas C (2010) Employment Fluctuations in a Dual Labor Market, Banco de España, Documento de Trabajo No. 1013
Decressin J, Fatás A (1995) Regional labor market dynamics in Europe. Eur Econ Rev 39(9):1627–1655
Dolado JJ, García-Serrano C, Jimeno JF (2002) Drawing lessons from the boom of temporary jobs in Spain. Econ J 112(480):270–295
Friedman M (1968) The role of monetary policy. Am Econ Rev 58(1):1–17
García-Cintado AC, Usabiaga C (2013) La Ley de Okun Española y la Lenta Salida de la Crisis Laboral. Documentación Social, forthcoming
García-Pérez JI, Osuna V (2012) Dual Labour Markets and the Tenure Distribution: Reducing Severance Pay or Introducing a Single Contract? FEDEA, Documento de Trabajo No. 2012-09
Gómez F, Usabiaga C (2001) Las Estimaciones del Desempleo de Equilibrio de la Economía Española: Una Panorámica. Revista de Economía Aplicada 9(27):103–129
Karanassou M, Snower DJ (1997) Is the natural rate a reference point? Eur Econ Rev 41(3–5):559–569
Karanassou M, Snower DJ (1998) How labour market flexibility affects unemployment: long-term implications of the chain reaction theory. Econ J 108(448):832–849
Layard R, Nickell S, Jackman R (1991) Unemployment, macroeconomic performance and the labour market. Oxford University Press, Oxford
Lee J, Strazicich MC (2003) Minimum Lagrange multiplier unit root test with two structural breaks. Rev Econ Stat 85(4):1082–1089
Lindbeck A, Snower DJ (1988) The insider-outsider theory of employment and unemployment. MIT Press, Cambridge
Maddala GS, Wu S (1999) A comparative study of unit root tests with panel data and a new simple test. Oxford Bull Econ Stat 61(s1):631–652
Nickell S, Nunziata L, Ochel W (2005) Unemployment in the OECD since the 1960s. What do we know? Econ J 115(500):1–27
O'Connell PGJ (1998) The overvaluation of purchasing power parity. J Int Econ 44(1):1–19
Phelps ES (1967) Phillips curves, expectations of inflation and optimal unemployment. Economica 34(135):254–281
Phelps ES (1968) Money-wage dynamics and labor-market equilibrium. J Polit Econ 76(s4):678–711
Phelps ES (1994) Structural slumps: the modern equilibrium theory of unemployment, interest and assets. Harvard University Press, Cambridge
Phelps ES, Zoega G (1998) Natural-Rate theory and OECD unemployment. Econ J 108(448):782–801
Romero-Ávila D, Usabiaga C (2007) Unit root tests, persistence and the unemployment rate of the US states. South Econ J 40(3):980–1007

Romero-Ávila D, Usabiaga C (2008) On the persistence of Spanish unemployment rates. Empir Econ 35(1):77–99
Romero-Ávila D, Usabiaga C (2009) The Unemployment paradigms revisited: a comparative analysis of US state and European unemployment. Contemp Econ Policy 27(3):321–334
Usabiaga C (2004) El Diferencial de Desempleo Andaluz. Aconcagua, Sevilla
Usabiaga C (2007) La Reforma del Mercado de Trabajo: El Caso Español. Papeles de Economía Española 111:177–197
Usabiaga C (2010) La Relación entre el Crecimiento, el Desempleo y el Empleo: El Caso Español. Cuadernos de Información Económica 214:83–88

Chapter 2
PANIC Analysis of Spanish Regional Unemployment

Abstract This chapter investigates the time series properties of the unemployment rate of the Spanish regions over the period 1976–2011. For that purpose, we employ the PANIC procedures of Bai and Ng (2004), which allows us to decompose the observed unemployment rate series into common factor and idiosyncratic components. This enables us to identify the exact source behind the hysteretic behaviour found in Spanish regional unemployment. Overall, our analysis with three different proxies for the excess of labour supply renders strong support for the hysteresis hypothesis, which appears to be caused by a common stochastic trend driving all the regional unemployment series.

Keywords Unemployment rate · Persistence · PANIC analysis · Common factor

2.1 Data

With regard to the unemployment rate, we employ three proxies for the excess of labour supply in the 17 Spanish regions: EPA unemployment rate –the most commonly used variable and the one to which we will be paying more attention–, SPEE unemployment rate and job-seekers rate. In the first place, we employ quarterly data on unemployment rates obtained by dividing the number of unemployed by the corresponding labour force figure over the period 1976(3)–2011(4). These data come from the EPA, which are provided by the National Statistical Office (Instituto Nacional de Estadística, INE). In the second place, we employ monthly data on unemployment rates based on registered or administrative unemployment ("paro registrado") figures for the period 1976(7)–2011(12). These data are supplied by the SPEE. In addition, we use a third proxy for the excess of labour supply also obtained from the SPEE for the period 1977(1)–2011(12), which focuses on the total number of persons looking for a job ("demandantes de

A. García-Cintado et al., *Spanish Regional Unemployment*, SpringerBriefs in Economics,
DOI: 10.1007/978-3-319-03686-1_2, © The Author(s) 2014

empleo")—we will denote this broader definition as "job-seekers".[1] All variables have been seasonally adjusted.[2]

It is important to note that we complement the empirical analysis using the EPA source with the SPEE data for several reasons. First, SPEE is the only official source that provides monthly data, so the series can be longer than those obtained from the EPA which is supplied on a quarterly basis; this fact can be relevant for the type of analysis that we implement in this work. Second, SPEE is a data source that has been used less frequently than the EPA or other international databases, so it is interesting to pay attention to this new line of results. Third, SPEE provides two additional proxies for the excess of labour supply, which allow us to check for the robustness of our findings with EPA data. Fourth, while in the first case survey data are provided (EPA), in the other the data stem from registration at a public institution (SPEE), two sources whose dynamics have not always followed the same path –see for example Garrido and Toharia (2004), and Pérez Infante (2006)–, thereby making this comparison appealing.

2.2 Econometric Methodology

The extant literature in the field has developed several second-generation panel unit root tests allowing for cross-correlation, which include the non-linear instrumental variables panel unit root test of Chang (2002), the five bootstrap panel unit root tests of Smith et al. (2004) and the Breitung and Das (2005) test. However, the problem with these tests is that they only allow for contemporaneous short-run cross-correlation, but not for stronger forms such as cross-sectional cointegration.

Breitung and Pesaran (2008) point out that the use of dynamic linear factor models can help make some parametric assumptions on the nature of the cross-sectional dependence and allow for much stronger forms of cross-dependence than bootstrap or nonlinear IV methods (Chang 2002). The panel procedures modelling cross-sectional dependence through a factor structure includes Pesaran (2007), Moon and Perron (2004) and Bai and Ng (2004). Pesaran (2007) only allows for one common factor, whereas Moon and Perron (2004) and Bai and Ng (2004) allow for multiple common factors. Of these three tests, Bai and Ng (2004) is

---

[1] This is a broader category than SPEE unemployment ("paro registrado") since it includes on-the-job search (intended to improve the labour status, to search for another job compatible with the current one, etc.), on-the-study search, agrarian workers receiving a special unemployment subsidy, especial temporary or part-time employment search, among other categories. Another SPEE proxy to which we could resort is non-occupied job seekers (DENOS being the Spanish acronym), an intermediate proxy between SPEE job seekers and registered unemployment rates.

[2] We keep up with the extant literature in the field by using seasonally adjusted data rather than unadjusted data. Our main results remain unchanged when we employ seasonally unadjusted data and are available from the authors upon request.

general enough to allow for cointegration across units, which implies that the observed series can contain common stochastic trends. Under these circumstances, the tests of Pesaran (2007) and Moon and Perron (2004) are likely to exhibit size distortions, since in the presence of cross-cointegration, the common trends may be confused with the common factors and hence removed from the data in the defactoring process. Therefore, if the remaining idiosyncratic component is stationary the test renders stationarity, despite the presence of one or several nonstationary common factors.[3]

Bai and Ng (2004) circumvent this caveat by developing the PANIC framework, which not only allows for nonstationary idiosyncratic components but also for common stochastic components. Let us model the observed data on regional unemployment rates as the sum of a deterministic part, a common component and an idiosyncratic error term:

$$U_{it} = D_{it} + \lambda_i' F_t + e_{it} \tag{1}$$

where λ_i is an $r \times 1$ vector of factor loadings, F_t is an $r \times 1$ vector of common factors, and e_{it} is the idiosyncratic component. D_{it} can contain a constant and a linear trend. Since λ_i and F_t can only be estimated consistently when $e_{it} \sim I(0)$, we estimate a model in first-differences like $\Delta U_{it} = \lambda_i' f_t + z_{it}$, where $z_{it} = \Delta e_{it}$ and $f_t = \Delta F_t$. As the next step we use principal components to estimate the common factors $\hat{f}_t$, the corresponding factor loadings $\hat{\lambda}_i$ and the residuals $\hat{z}_{it} = y_{it} - \hat{\lambda}_i' \hat{f}_t$, thereby preserving the order of integration of F_t and e_{it}. We follow Bai and Ng (2002) by normalising U_{it} for each cross-section unit to have a unit variance. We then recumulate the common factors and the residuals as follows: $\hat{F}_t = \sum_{s=2}^{t} \hat{f}_s$ and $\hat{e}_{it} = \sum_{s=2}^{t} \hat{z}_{is}$, which can be used to test for a unit root in the common and idiosyncratic components, respectively.

Before conducting the tests for a unit root in the common and idiosyncratic components, it is necessary to determine the number of common factors. This is done through the BIC_3 information criterion that takes the form:

$$BIC_3(k) = \hat{\sigma}_e^2(k) + k\hat{\sigma}_e^2(k_{\max})\left(\frac{(N+T-k)\ln(NT)}{NT}\right) \tag{2}$$

where k is the number of factors included in the model, $\hat{\sigma}_e^2(k)$ is the variance of the estimated idiosyncratic components, and $\hat{\sigma}_e^2(k_{\max})$ is the variance of the idiosyncratic components estimated with the maximum number of factors ($k_{max} = 5$). As pointed out by Bai and Ng (2002), the second argument in the loss function represents the penalty for overfitting, which is thought to correct for the fact that

---

[3] An additional advantage of using this framework is that, whereas the application of other panel unit root tests with a factor structure such as those of Moon and Perron (2004) and Pesaran (2007) assumes that both common and idiosyncratic components have the same order of integration, the PANIC approach is flexible enough as to allow for a different order of integration in the common factor(s) and idiosyncratic components.

models with a larger number of factors can fit at least as good as models with fewer common factors, but efficiency is reduced as more factor loading parameters are being estimated. We choose the optimal number of common factors $\hat{k}$ as $\arg\min_{0\leq k\leq 5} BIC_3(k)$. Our preferred criterion is BIC_3 because Bai and Ng (2002, pp. 205–207) showed that for a sufficiently general scenario in which the idiosyncratic errors can be serially correlated and cross-correlated, the BIC_3 criterion exhibits very good properties (see Tables VII and VIII in Bai and Ng 2002). Besides, Moon and Perron (2007, p. 387) stress that the BIC_3 criterion "performs better in selecting the number of factors when min(*N,T*) is small (≤ 20), as is often the case in empirical applications". Notwithstanding, for the sake of robustness, we also compute the IC_1, IC_2 and IC_3 panel information criteria proposed by Bai and Ng (2002), which have the advantage over the PC_p counterparts that they do not depend on the maximum number of factors. The three IC_p criteria are represented by $\ln(\hat{\sigma}_e^2(k)) + kg(N,T)$, with $g(N,T)$ being a penalty function that depends on both *T* and *N*. This penalty function equals $\left(\frac{N+T}{NT}\right)\ln\left(\frac{NT}{N+T}\right)$, $\left(\frac{N+T}{NT}\right)\ln\left(C_{NT}^2\right)$ and $\frac{\ln C_{NT}^2}{C_{NT}^2}$ for IC_1, IC_2 and IC_3 respectively, where $C_{NT}^2 = \min(N,T)$.

To test for a unit root in the idiosyncratic components, Bai and Ng (2004) estimate standard Augmented Dickey-Fuller (ADF) specifications of the following form:

$$\Delta\hat{e}_{it} = \delta_{i,0}\hat{e}_{i,t-1} + \sum_{j=1}^{p_i}\delta_{i,j}\Delta\hat{e}_{i,t-j} + u_{it} \tag{3}$$

They then employ the ADF t-statistic for testing $\delta_{i,0} = 0$, which is denoted by $ADF_{\hat{e}}^{c}(i)$ or $ADF_{\hat{e}}^{\tau}(i)$ for the cases of only constant and constant and linear trend in specification (1), respectively.[4] To raise statistical power, Bai and Ng (2004) recommend employing pooled statistics based on the Fisher-type inverse Chi-square tests of Maddala and Wu (1999) and Choi (2001), only for the case in which the idiosyncratic components are found to be independent across cross-sectional units.[5] Letting $\pi_{\hat{e}}^{c}(i)$ be the *p*-value associated with $ADF_{\hat{e}}^{c}(i)$, we have[6]:

---

[4] The asymptotic distribution of $ADF_{\hat{e}}^{c}(i)$ coincides with the Dickey-Fuller (DF) distribution for the case of no constant, while that of $ADF_{\hat{e}}^{\tau}(i)$ is proportional to the reciprocal of a Brownian bridge.

[5] If the observed series are correctly decomposed into the common and idiosyncratic components, the latter (i.e. the defactored data) should by assumption be cross-sectionally independent. The PANIC approach has the further advantage that the common factors and indiosyncratic components are estimated consistently irrespective of their order of integration.

[6] The same holds for the case of a trend, where $\pi_{\hat{e}}^{\tau}(i)$ is the *p*-value associated with $ADF_{\hat{e}}^{\tau}(i)$. The pooled statistics for the trend specification are denoted as $P_{\hat{e}}^{\tau}$ and $Z_{\hat{e}}^{\tau}$. We should point out that under a factor structure, it is not appropriate to pool individual unit root tests for the observed series, since the limiting distribution of the test would contain terms that are common across cross-sectional units. In contrast, "pooling of tests for $\hat{e}_{it}$ is asymptotically valid under the more plausible assumption that $\hat{e}_{it}$ is independent across *i*" (Bai and Ng 2004, p. 1140).

$$P_{\hat{e}}^{c} = -2\sum_{i=1}^{N} \log \pi_{\hat{e}}^{c}(i) \xrightarrow{d} \chi^{2}_{(2N)} \text{for } N \quad \text{fixed}, \quad T \to \infty, \tag{4}$$

$$Z_{\hat{e}}^{c} = \frac{-\sum_{i=1}^{N} \log \pi_{\hat{e}}^{c}(i) - N}{\sqrt{N}} \xrightarrow{d} N(0,1) \quad \text{for} \quad N, T \to \infty. \tag{5}$$

To test for nonstationarity in the common factors, Bai and Ng (2004) propose to use an ADF test for the case of a single common factor ($k = 1$) or a rank test when $k > 1$. In the former case, they estimate an ADF specification for $\hat{F}_t$ with the same deterministic components as in model (1):

$$\Delta\hat{F}_t = D_t + \gamma_{i,0}\hat{F}_{t-1} + \sum_{j=1}^{p} \gamma_{i,j}\Delta\hat{F}_{t-j} + v_{it} \tag{6}$$

The corresponding ADF t-statistics are denoted by $ADF_{\hat{F}}^{c}$ and $ADF_{\hat{F}}^{\tau}$ and are characterised by the limiting distribution of the Dickey and Fuller (1979) test for the specifications with only a constant, and a constant and a trend, respectively. For the case of multiple common factors, the number of common stochastic trends in the common factors are determined using the modified rank tests given by the filter test MQ_f and the corrected test MQ_c.

2.3 Empirical Results

Once we have presented a brief description of the econometric methodology behind the PANIC approach, we now shift the focus to report the results obtained from its application. There are two reasons why we apply the testing procedures of Bai and Ng (2004). The testing procedures of Smith et al. (2004), Breitung and Das (2005), the bootstrap version of Hadri (2000) and Carrión-i-Silvestre et al. (2005) (i) only allow for weak forms of cross-sectional dependence, which exclude for instance the existence of cross-sectional cointegration and (ii) provide strong evidence of a unit root in Spanish regional unemployment (see Romero-Ávila and Usabiaga 2008). Therefore, as there is strong evidence in the extant literature supporting the presence of a unit root in Spanish regional unemployment, it is necessary to establish the source of nonstationarity, i.e. whether it is present in the idiosyncratic components and/or in the common factors.

Before conducting the PANIC analysis, we carry out a formal analysis of the prevalence of cross-sectional dependence in regional unemployment rate innovations by applying the tests for cross-dependence developed by Breusch and Pagan (1980) and Pesaran (2004).[7] It is remarkable that the LM test of Breusch and

[7] The latter is based on the average of pair-wise correlation coefficients ($\hat{\rho}_{ij}$) of ordinary least squares (OLS) residuals obtained from standard ADF regressions for each individual. The order

Table 2.1 Information criteria. EPA unemployment rate

Number of factors (k)	IC_1 (k)	IC_2 (k)	IC_3 (k)	BIC_3 (k)
0	−0.0193	−0.0193	−0.0193	0.9809
1	−0.3419	−0.3343*	−0.3544	0.7469*
2	−0.3488*	−0.3338	−0.3740*	0.7971
3	−0.3188	−0.2963	−0.3566	0.8779
4	−0.3098	−0.2798	−0.3602	0.9586
5	−0.3069	−0.2694	−0.3699	1.0459

Note * represents the lowest value of the information criteria. See the text for the equations associated with the information criteria
Source Own elaboration

Pagan (1980) equals 67.21 and 69.42 for the specifications without and with trends, and the respective values of the CD test of Pesaran (2004) are 32.36 and 46.39. In all cases, we reject the null hypothesis of cross-sectionally independent errors at the 1 % level of significance, which supports the use of PANIC that allows for cross-sectional dependence so that large size distortions in the tests are avoided.

Prior to testing for a unit root in the idiosyncratic series and common factors, we need to estimate the factors through principal components and then select the number of common factors present in the panel containing the unemployment rates of the 17 regions. As noted above, this is done with the BIC_3 procedure developed in Bai and Ng (2002), which appears to perform better than alternative information criteria. Setting a maximum number of factors equal to five, the BIC_3 criterion selects one common factor. Table 2.1 presents the results for the EPA unemployment rate. For the sake of robustness, the table also reports the results from the three panel information criteria (IC_p) proposed by Bai and Ng (2002), which appear to favour the existence of either one or two common factors. Since Bai and Ng (2002) found evidence that the BIC_3 criterion performed remarkably well in the presence of cross-sectional dependence and (Gengenbach et al. 2010, p. 134) provided simulation evidence of the superior performance of the BIC_3 criterion for short-N panels, and given the difficulty in determining the number of common factors in panels with a relatively short N-dimension, we will conduct the decomposition of the unemployment rate series into common and idiosyncratic

(Footnote 7 continued)
of the autoregressive model is selected using the *t-sig* criterion in Ng and Perron (1995), with the maximum number of lags set at $p = 4(T/100)^{1/4}$. Pesaran's test is given by $CD = \sqrt{2T/(N(N-1))}\left(\sum_{i=1}^{N-1}\sum_{j=i+1}^{N}\hat{\rho}_{ij}\right)\xrightarrow{d}N(0,1)$. The CD statistic tests the null hypothesis of cross-sectional independence, is distributed as a two-tailed standard normal distribution and exhibits good finite-sample properties. In addition, Breusch and Pagan (1980) test the null hypothesis of cross-sectionally independent errors via the following Lagrange Multiplier (LM) statistic $CD_{lm} = T\sum_{i=1}^{N-1}\sum_{j=i+1}^{N}\hat{\rho}_{ij}^2 \xrightarrow{d} \chi^2_{N(N-1)/2}$.

components as if there was one common factor.[8] Furthermore, we apply the IPC_1, IPC_2 and IPC_3 information criteria of Bai (2004) to determine the number of *non-stationary* common factors in the panel (setting the maximum number of factors to five), which clearly support the existence of only one common stochastic factor (exactly the result found below with the $ADF_{\hat{F}}^{c}$ and $ADF_{\hat{F}}^{\tau}$ statistics).[9] Therefore, if we find the common factor to be nonstationary and the idiosyncratic components to be stationary, there would be evidence of pair-wise cointegration among the 17 regional unemployment rates forming the panel. This would imply that regional unemployment rates would be tightly linked with one another due to the existence of a common stochastic trend driving them all.

Table 2.2 reports the results of the univariate and pooled ADF statistics for both the observed unemployment rate series (column 3) and the idiosyncratic components (column 4) in addition to the ADF statistic for the common factor for the EPA unemployment rate. For the sake of robustness, we present the results for the specification with and without trends, though we admit that the specification with no deterministic trends may be more meaningful for the analysis of unemployment rates. Indeed, Fig. 2.1 shown below presents rather limited evidence of trending behaviour in Spanish regional unemployment. Remarkably, throughout the PANIC analysis, the same results are obtained irrespective of the inclusion of deterministic trends in the specification. Therefore, even though the tables present the results including and excluding deterministic trends, when commenting the results we focus on the specification without trends.[10]

As reported in column 3 of Table 2.2, direct testing for a unit root in the observed data provides clear-cut evidence of non-stationarity with the univariate ADF statistics, since we are only able to reject the nonstationarity null hypothesis

[8] Note also that even though the information criteria for determining the optimal number of common factors work reasonably well in simulations, their practical application is difficult since they are usually found to select the maximum number of common factors allowed (Gengenbach et al. 2010, p. 219). Nevertheless, given that the four information criteria select either one or two common factors, which are much lower than the maximum number permitted, we are confident that the optimal number of common factors is correctly estimated.

[9] Unlike the Bai and Ng (2004) information criteria for selecting the optimal number of common factors (stationary and non-stationary) that applies to first-differenced data, the IPC_p panel information criteria of Bai (2004) for determining the number of *non-stationary* common factors is applied to level data. The consistency of the IPC_p information criteria requires the idiosyncratic component to be I(0), result that we find below.

[10] We also tested the unit root hypothesis with the tests of Pesaran (2007) and Moon and Perron (2004) and we could reject the unit root null hypothesis at the 1 % for the latter for the specification without trends ($t_a^* = -11.42, t_b^* = -4.93$, and CIPS = –1.73), and fail to do so for the specification with trends for all these tests ($t_a^* = -0.047, t_b^* = -0.051$, and CIPS = −2.46). As noted above, the rejection of the nonstationarity null with the Moon and Perron (2004) tests for the no-trend specification should not be surprising, since they exhibit large size distortions in the presence of cross-cointegration, because the common trends are confused with the common factors and hence removed from the data in the defactoring process.

Table 2.2 Panel analysis of nonstationarity in idiosyncratic and common components of EPA unemployment rate

	No trend specification			Trend specification				
Region	k	$ADF_y^c(i)$	$ADF_{\hat{e}}^c(i)$	k	$ADF_y^\tau(i)$	$ADF_{\hat{e}}^\tau(i)$	$\frac{\sigma(\Delta\hat{e}_{it})}{\sigma(\Delta y_{it})}$	$\frac{\sigma(\lambda_i' F_t)}{\sigma(\hat{e}_{it})}$
Andalusia	3	−2.491	−1.838*	2	−2.514	−1.831	0.477	3.478
Aragon	5	−2.529	−1.861*	5	−2.589	−1.740	0.636	2.819
Asturias	3	−2.190	−2.088**	4	−2.240	−1.994	0.573	2.937
Balearic Islands	8	−1.257	−0.250	8	−1.331	−1.105	0.702	1.819
Basque Country	6	−2.009	−0.081	6	−2.856	−3.714***	0.610	0.974
Canary Islands	8	−1.567	−1.490	8	−1.542	−1.400	0.626	1.937
Cantabria	2	−2.301	−1.184	2	−2.369	−1.087	0.651	2.256
Castilla Leon	8	−2.450	−1.185	8	−2.471	−0.600	0.379	2.962
Castilla-La Mancha	4	−1.847	−0.435	4	−1.890	−1.372	0.462	2.887
Catalonia	2	−2.585*	−2.174**	2	−2.694	−2.673**	0.551	1.785
Extremadura	8	−2.079	−2.206**	8	−2.093	−2.174	0.524	2.653
Galicia	3	−2.213	−1.539	3	−2.369	−1.298	0.644	1.221
Madrid	2	−2.387	−2.013	2	−2.354	−2.099	0.541	2.384
Murcia	5	−2.534	−1.568	2	−2.536	−1.817	0.729	2.693
Navarra	5	−2.022	−1.162	5	−2.315	−1.866	0.840	1.100
Rioja	7	−2.522	−2.164**	0	−2.518	−2.292	0.708	3.197
Valencian Community	3	−2.244	−1.747*	3	−2.249	−2.056	0.464	3.335
Critical values								
1 %		−3.430	−2.580		−3.960	−3.167		
5 %		−2.860	−1.950		−3.410	−2.577		
10 %		−2.570	−1.620		−3.120	−2.314		

(continued)

Table 2.2 (continued)

Region	No trend specification			Trend specification				
	k	$ADF_y^c(i)$	$ADF_{\hat{e}}^c(i)$	k	$ADF_y^\tau(i)$	$ADF_{\hat{e}}^\tau(i)$	$\frac{\sigma(\Delta\hat{e}_{it})}{\sigma(\Delta y_{it})}$	$\frac{\sigma(\lambda_i' F_t)}{\sigma(\hat{e}_{it})}$
Pooled statistics								
		$P_{\hat{e}}^c$	76.959***		$P_{\hat{e}}^\tau$	53.762**		
		$Z_{\hat{e}}^c$	5.210***		$Z_{\hat{e}}^\tau$	2.397***		

Common factor analysis		Critical values					Critical values		
Statistic		1 %	5 %	10 %	Statistic		1 %	5 %	10 %
$ADF_{\hat{F}}^c$	−2.313	−3.430	−2.860	−2.570	$ADF_{\hat{F}}^\tau$	−2.305	−3.960	−3.410	−3.120

Note The augmented autoregressions employed in the ADF analysis set a maximum lag-order equal to $p = 4(T/100)^{1/4}$. The information criterion BIC_3 has chosen an optimal rank equal to 1 for the tests of Bai and Ng (2004). $P_{\hat{e}}$ is distributed as χ^2_{34}, with 1 %, 5 % and 10 % critical values equal to 56.061, 48.602 and 44.903, respectively. $Z_{\hat{e}}$ is distributed as N(0, 1) with 1 %, 5 % and 10 % critical values equal to 2.326, 1.645 and 1.282. ***, ** and * imply rejection of the null hypothesis at 1 %, 5 % and 10 %, respectively

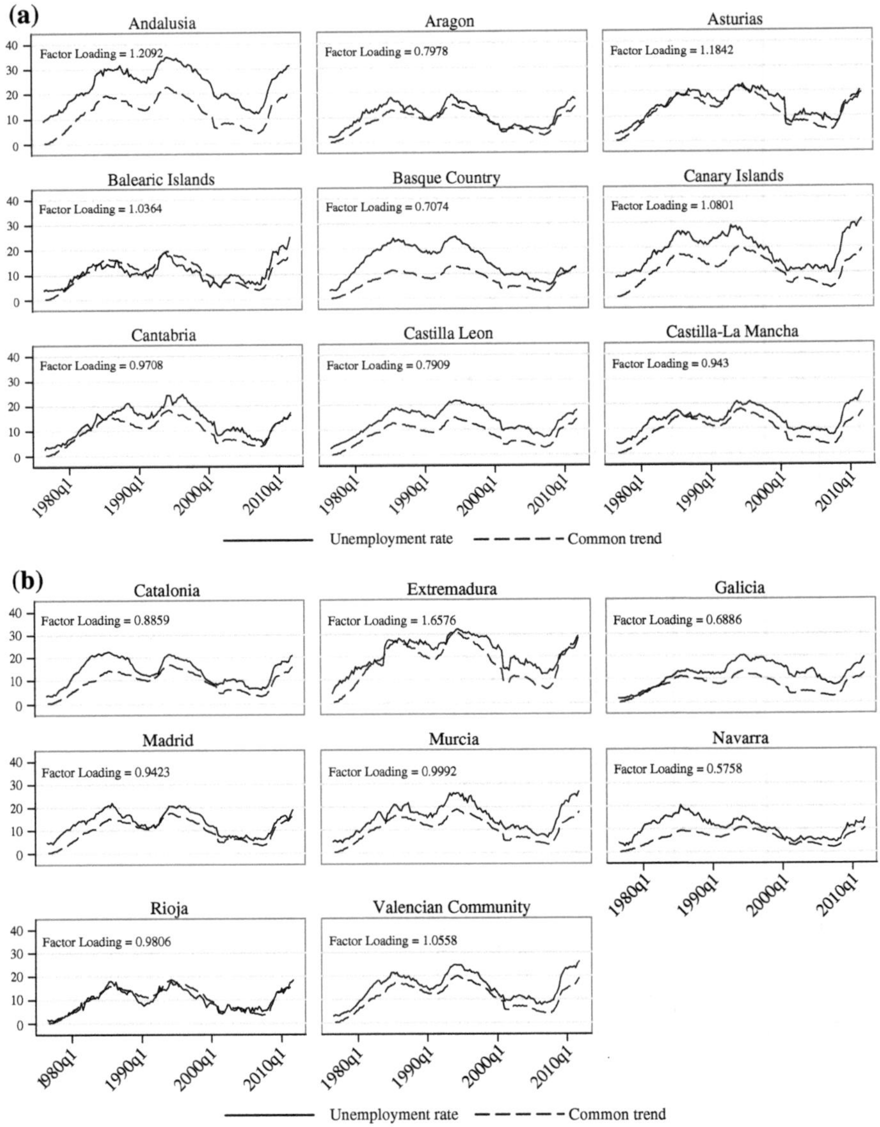

Fig. 2.1 **a** Regional EPA unemployment rates and the common trend. **b** Regional EPA unemployment rates and the common trend

for Catalonia at the 10 % level.[11] Therefore, the next step is to determine whether the nonstationary behaviour of Spanish regional unemployment is caused by the

[11] As pointed out above, the presence of cross-sectional dependence prevents us from reporting the pooled ADF statistics associated with the observed unemployment rate series.

common factor and/or the idiosyncratic component. Column 4 presents the univariate ADF statistic as well as the pooled statistics based on the Fisher-type inverse Chi-square tests of Maddala and Wu (1999) and Choi (2001) for testing the unit root null hypothesis for the idiosyncratic components. Univariate evidence from the application of the ADF statistic indicates that the unit root hypothesis can be rejected for seven regions at conventional significance levels: Asturias, Catalonia, Extremadura and Rioja at the 5 % level, and Andalusia, Aragon and Valencian Community at the 10 % level. The fact that the pooled statistics are able to reject the joint nonstationarity null at the 1 % significance level indicates that the idiosyncratic components are jointly stationary.

Regarding the analysis of the time series properties of the common factor, the ADF statistic for the common factor is presented in the bottom part of the table. It is remarkable that the ADF test for a unit root in the common factor fails to reject the null even at the 10 % level.[12] Hence, the above decomposition of the original series into the idiosyncratic and common components indicates that the source of nonstationarity is primarily a common stochastic trend which drives the nonstationarity in the observed unemployment rate series. This, coupled with the existence of jointly stationary idiosyncratic components, provides evidence of pairwise cointegration across Spanish regional unemployment rates.

From Fig. 2.1 we observe that it is not surprising our finding of a common stochastic trend driving the time series behaviour of Spanish regional unemployment rates. In fact, both series exhibit a similar evolution and expectedly similar nonstationarity properties over the 35-year period under scrutiny. It is also remarkable that a simple common stochastic factor along with a vector of factor loadings can track so closely the evolution of each of the 17 regional unemployment rate series. Since the difference between both series constitutes the idiosyncratic component, it is not surprising either that we previously obtained evidence of stationarity in the idiosyncratic part, thus accounting for the transitory fluctuations that unemployment rates exhibit over time (as deviations of regional unemployment rates from the common trend).

In columns 8 and 9 of Table 2.2 we show the ratio of the standard deviation of the idiosyncratic component to the standard deviation of the observed data (both expressed in first-differences) as well as the standard deviation of the common to the idiosyncratic component, respectively. These statistics help us determine the relative importance of the common and idiosyncratic components. If the first ratio is close to one and the second is relatively small, region-specific variations would prevail. In relative terms, this appears to be the case for Navarra and to a lower extent Galicia and the Basque Country, which are mainly driven by idiosyncratic variations while other regions' unemployment rates are (to a differing degree) more affected by common factors.

The detailed results shown in the Appendix for the SPEE unemployment rate and the job seekers rate are largely the same as those presented in Table 2.2 for the

[12] The same results essentially follow for the specification with a trend.

EPA unemployment rate. Even though the BIC_3 criterion indicates the existence of three and two common factors for the SPEE unemployment rate and job-seekers rate, respectively, the application of the improved IPC_1, IPC_2 and IPC_3 information criteria of Bai (2004) clearly indicates the existence of only one common stochastic factor in the series, which exactly coincides with the findings for the EPA unemployment rate.[13] As with the EPA unemployment rate, not only does the common factor appear to be clearly nonstationary but also are the idiosyncratic components found to be jointly stationary when employing the Fisher-type inverse Chi-square pooled statistics. In addition, at the univariate level, the ADF statistic provides even higher evidence of stationarity in individual idiosyncratic series than in Table 2.2 since the unit root null appears rejected in all regions except for Andalusia, the Basque Country, Castilla-La Mancha and Navarra (see column 4 of Table A3).[14]

All in all, our thorough analysis of the stochastic properties of our panel of Spanish regional unemployment rates provides strong evidence for the presence of hysteretic behaviour in unemployment caused by the presence of a nonstationary common factor. This finding coupled with the existence of stationary idiosyncratic components implies the existence of pairwise cointegration among the 17 regional unemployment rates, largely due to the presence of a common stochastic trend closely linking the regional unemployment rate series with one another.

Given the importance of the above result, the next chapter is devoted to the identification of the macroeconomic and/or institutional factors characterising the common stochastic trend which drives regional unemployment rates. By determining the factors responsible for such common hysteretic patterns in Spanish unemployment, we will be able to propose ideas and a policy bundle to try to combat the sources of hysteresis in Spanish unemployment.

References

Bai J (2004) Estimating cross-section common stochastic trends in non-stationary panel data. J Econometrics 122(1):137–183

Bai J, Ng S (2002) Determining the number of factors in approximate factor models. Econometrica 70(1):191–221

Bai J, Ng S (2004) A PANIC attack on unit roots and cointegration. Econometrica 72(4):1127–1177

Breitung J, Das S (2005) Panel unit root tests under cross-sectional dependence. Stat Neerl 59(4):414–433

[13] Since the IC_p and BIC_3 criteria may not appear to perform optimally for small-N panels, and considering that the IPC_p criteria favour the presence of one common stochastic factor, we present the results of the PANIC analysis for these two proxies assuming the existence of only one common factor, though highlighting that the PANIC main results are fairly robust to considering three and two common factors in the respective SPEE excess labour supply measures.

[14] As far as the idiosyncratic series associated with the job seekers rate, the ADF statistic rejects the unit root null at the 10 % or better for 10 regions.

Breitung J, Pesaran MH (2008) Unit roots and cointegration in panels. In: Matyas L, Sevestre P (eds) The econometrics of panel data: fundamentals and recent developments in theory and practice. Kluwer Academic Publishers, Dordrecht, pp 279–322

Breusch TS, Pagan AR (1980) The lagrange multiplier test and its application to model specifications in econometrics. Rev Econ Stud 47(1):239–253

Carrión-i-Silvestre JL, Del Barrio T, López-Bazo E (2005) Breaking the panels: an application to the GDP per capita. Econometrics J 8(2):159–175

Chang Y (2002) Nonlinear IV unit root tests in panels with cross-sectional dependency. J Econometrics 110(2):261–292

Choi I (2001) Unit root tests for panel data. J Int Money Finance 20(2):249–272

Dickey DA, Fuller WA (1979) Distribution of the estimators for autoregressive time series with a unit root. J Am Stat Assoc 74(366):427–431

Garrido L, Toharia L (2004) What does it take to be (counted as) unemployed? the case of Spain. Labour Econ 11(4):507–523

Gengenbach C, Palm FC, Urbain JP (2010) Panel unit root tests in the presence of cross-sectional dependencies: comparisons and implications for modelling. Econometric Rev 29(2):111–145

Hadri K (2000) Testing for stationarity in heterogeneous panel data. Econometrics J 3(2):148–161

Maddala GS, Wu S (1999) A comparative study of unit root tests with panel data and a new simple test. Oxford Bull Econ Stat 61(s1):631–652

Moon HR, Perron B (2004) Testing for a unit root in panels with dynamic factors. J Econometrics 122(1):81–126

Moon HR, Perron B (2007) An empirical analysis of non-stationarity in a panel of interest rates with factors. J Appl Econometrics 22(2):383–400

Ng S, Perron P (1995) Unit root tests in ARMA models with data-dependent methods for the selection of the truncation lag. J Am Stat Assoc 90(429):268-281

Pérez Infante JI (2006) Las Estadísticas del Mercado de Trabajo en España. Ministerio de Trabajo y Asuntos Sociales, Madrid

Pesaran MH (2004) General diagnostic tests for cross section dependence in panels. Institute for the Study of Labor (IZA), Discussion Paper No. 1240

Pesaran MH (2007) A simple panel unit root test in the presence of cross-section dependence. J Appl Econometrics 22(2):265–312

Romero-Ávila D, Usabiaga C (2008) On the persistence of Spanish unemployment rates. Empir Econ 35(1):77–99

Smith LV, Leybourne S, Kim T, Newbold P (2004) More powerful panel data unit root tests with an application to mean reversion in real exchange rates. J Appl Econometrics 19(2):147–170

Chapter 3
Explaining the Common Stochastic Trend in Spanish Regional Unemployment: Granger-Causality Analysis

Abstract This chapter delves deeper into the likely sources of Spanish unemployment by making use of a broad collection of institutional and macroeconomic variables which, the economic literature suggests, can exert an influence on unemployment. Specifically, we focus on studying whether each variable individually considered Granger-causes the common factor of the unemployment rate and find that there is a wide range of macroeconomic and institutional variables that might be useful for anticipating a change in the unemployment rate. By determining the factors responsible for the common hysteretic patterns in Spanish unemployment, we will be in a position to suggest policies that can help tackle this problem.

Keywords Unemployment rate · Granger-causality · Vector autoregression

3.1 Data and Empirical Approach

In this section we set out to delve deeper into the likely sources of Spanish unemployment by making use of a broad collection of institutional and macroeconomic variables which, the economic literature suggests, can exert an influence over the former in the short, medium and long run. Specifically, we focus on studying whether each variable individually considered Granger-causes the common factor of the unemployment rate and find that there is a wide range of macroeconomic and institutional variables that might be useful for anticipating a change in the unemployment rate.

Before proceeding with the Granger-causality analysis, we test for a unit root in the macroeconomic variables employed to explain the common stochastic trend in Spanish regional unemployment.[1] The univariate unit root tests employed are the

[1] Note that we focus exclusively on the direction of causality going from the different macroeconomic and institutional variables to the common factor.

A. García-Cintado et al., *Spanish Regional Unemployment*, SpringerBriefs in Economics,
DOI: 10.1007/978-3-319-03686-1_3,

ADF t-statistic of Dickey and Fuller (1979), the ADF^{GLS} and the feasible point optimal test of Elliot et al. (1996), and the efficient modified Phillips-Perron tests of Ng and Perron (2001).[2] In order to overcome the possibility of spurious regression problems, the Granger-causality test between individual variables and the stochastic common factor is conducted with stationary variables. For that purpose, first-differences are applied to the stochastic common factor and those explanatory variables found to be I(1). Likewise, those explanatory variables that are I(2) will be differenced twice.

As stated earlier, the database with which we work is quite large and comprises 88 variables, which, according to economic theory, can be thought of as affecting the unemployment rate in the short, medium and long run. It is important to stress that if one is to detect what variables could potentially determine the core unemployment rate, falling back on the macroeconomic and institutional variables the economic literature puts forth as the likely causes of long-term unemployment rate appears to be mandatory. This is why, in addition to employing macroeconomic variables, like Gross Domestic Product (GDP), GDP Growth, Public Spending, Rate of Money Growth in Real Terms, Real Interest Rate, Real Exchange Rate, Oil Price, etc., we also deal with a set of institutional variables, such as Union Density, Union Coverage, Unemployment Benefits, Employment Protection, Active Labour Market Policies (ALMPs), etc. The sources on which we draw are diverse: OECD databases, International Financial Statistics (IFS) database, World Economic Outlook database, World Development Indicators, INE, Banco de España (BdE), EUKLEMS, BDMORES, BDREMS, CESifo, FRDB-IZA database, ICTWSS database, among others.[3]

Moreover, it must also be acknowledged that our analysis does not allow us to address interactions between these macroeconomic and institutional variables, or between macroeconomic shocks and institutions, approach that an influential strand of the literature has popularised (see for example Blanchard and Wolfers 2000; for an application to Spain, see for example Bentolila and Jimeno 2006).

All the data are shown in levels –although some variables expressed in rates of change are used as well– and on a quarterly basis, and have been seasonally adjusted when necessary. Table 3.1 below displays only those variables that appear to explain the common factor with the Granger-causality analysis.[4] We just concentrate on the short-run relationships and, for clarification purposes, sort the Granger-causality results into different categories depending on the nature of each variable. Thus, the variables considered could be grouped as follows:

---

[2] When the degree of integration differs according to the different test, we compute the Granger-causality analysis under the different scenarios and the results remain fairly unaltered.

[3] See exact data sources for each of the explanatory variables in Table A1 in the Appendix.

[4] In Table A5 in the Appendix, we provide the Granger-causality analysis results for all the variables investigated, including all those variables that do not significantly Granger-cause the common factor driving Spanish regional unemployment rates.

Table 3.1 Granger-causality analysis

Variables	Statistical significance (%)	*P*-value
Labour productivity	10	0.0639
Total factor productivity growth	10	0.0805
Housing prices	1	0.0005
M3	5	0.0430
Real per capita GDP	1	0.0000
Real gross value added	1	0.0000
GDP growth (OECD)	10	0.0746
Current account (% of GDP) OECD	1	0.0000
Current account (% of GDP) IMF	1	0.0000
Net international investment position (NIIP)	5	0.0336
Trade (% of GDP)	10	0.0899
Capital stock (% of GDP) BDREMS	5	0.0246
Gross fixed capital formation (% of GDP) WDI	1	0.0000
Gross fixed capital formation (% of GDP) BDREMS	1	0.0002
Public spending (% of GDP)	1	0.0004
Public revenue (% of GDP)	10	0.0555
Tax revenue (% of GDP)	5	0.0267
Government net borrowing lending OECD	1	0.0000
Government net borrowing lending IMF	1	0.0001
Government debt (% of GDP)	1	0.0000
Employment rate	1	0.0000
Labor participation rate	1	0.0036
Labor market tightness (vacancies/unemployment)	1	0.0000
ULCs index	5	0.0126
ULC growth	1	0.0032
Ordinary wage cost	10	0.0879
Total wage cost	1	0.0061
Mean wage	1	0.0000
Ratio of minimum wage to mean wage	1	0.0050
Workers 16–24 (% of total workers)	10	0.0920
Agriculture sector workers (% of total workers)	5	0.0105
Construction sector workers (% of total workers)	1	0.0001
Services sector workers (% of total workers)	1	0.0063
Female workers (% of total workers)	1	0.0061
Male workers (% of total workers)	1	0.0061
Oil price (US$)	1	0.0013
Oil price (€)	5	0.0196
Energy price index	1	0.0021
Employment protection	1	0.0051
Urban (%)	5	0.0413
Bargaining (or union) coverage	10	0.0983
Active labour market policies	1	0.0004
Human capital	1	0.0076
Unemployment benefits gross replacement rate (average)	1	0.0022
Benefit duration index	1	0.0005

(1) Real production variables, which comprise Labour Productivity, Total Factor Productivity (TFP) growth, Real Per Capita GDP, Gross Value Added at constant prices (GVA), GDP growth, Capital Stock (as a percentage of GDP) and Gross Fixed Capital Formation –GFCF– (as a percentage of GDP).
(2) Open economy variables, consisting of Current Account Balance (as a percentage of GDP), International Trade (as a percentage of GDP) and Net International Investment Position (NIIP).
(3) Fiscal variables, which include Public Spending (as a percentage of GDP), Public Revenue (as a percentage of GDP), Tax Revenue (as a percentage of GDP), Public Deficit (as a percentage of GDP) and Public Debt (as a percentage of GDP).
(4) Monetary variables, such as Money Supply (M3).
(5) Labour variables, like Employment Rate, Inactivity Rate, Labour Market Tightness (Vacancies/Unemployment ratio), Workers aged 16–24 (as a percentage of Total Workers), Agriculture Sector Workers (as a percentage of Total Workers), Construction Sector Workers (as a percentage of Total Workers), Services Sector Workers (as a percentage of Total Workers) and Female Workers (as a percentage of Total Workers).
(6) Labour cost variables, these being Unit Labour Cost (ULC) Index, ULC growth, Total Wage Cost, Mean Wage and Ratio of Minimum Wage to Mean Wage.
(7) Price variables, whose representatives in our sample are Housing Prices, Oil Price (both in US Dollars and in Euros) and Energy Price Index.
(8) Institutional variables, encompassing Employment Protection, Union Coverage, ALMPs, Unemployment Benefit Duration Index, Human Capital, Urban Population, and Gross Unemployment Benefit Replacement Rate (two-year average).

3.2 Empirical Results

3.2.1 Real Production Variables

It seems straightforward to think of real production variables as affecting the unemployment rate. That is precisely what we run into in our analysis. From a theoretical standpoint, GDP growth –provided that it exceeds a given threshold– should be expected to reduce short-term unemployment. This relationship is referred to as Okun's law in the macroeconomic literature –see for example Crespo-Cuaresma (2003). For the case of Spain, most studies stress the extraordinary high value of the coefficient in the relationship, i.e. the effect of a 1 % change in output on the unemployment rate –see Usabiaga (2010) and García-Cintado and Usabiaga (2013). Ball et al. (2013) for example estimate a coefficient of −0.85 (for the sake of comparison, the US coefficient is estimated to be −0.45). This anomalously high value, upon which many researchers agree, can be attributed to the fact that Spain-based firms lean toward an excessive use of fixed-term labour contracts when making the decision of hiring workers (Dolado et al. 2002). We utilise several measures of real output: Per capita Real GDP and GDP growth, as provided by the OECD databases, which Granger-cause the common factor at the 1 % and 10 % levels of significance, respectively, and GVA, which appears significant at the 1 % level.

Still within this first group, Labour Productivity and TFP growth are also found to explain the common factor both at the 10 %. Much has been written over the past decades about the link between TFP growth and unemployment, but no unanimous conclusion appears to have been reached so far (a good simple account is Blanchard et al. 1995). In principle, a positive TFP shock could affect the unemployment rate differently—in either direction—depending on the level of aggregate demand, on whether we are in the short or in the long run and on the set of institutions in place in the country. In the short run, unemployment can go up as a result of a positive technological shock. Calibrated Real Business Cycle (RBC) models indeed show that unemployment (hours worked) may increase (decline) when a positive TFP shock arises (see Galí and Rabanal 2004). Blanchard (2000) employs a simple model whereby he demonstrates that a decline in the rate of technological progress should cause a temporary rise in equilibrium unemployment until workers and firms realise that TFP growth has diminished and moderate their wage and price demands. Once this moderation has set in, the unemployment rate should be expected to return to its initial long-run equilibrium value.[5]

As for Labour Productivity, the widely accepted saying "Spain is different" fits in rather well in this context, since it is one of the few industrialised countries whose aggregate labour productivity follows a severe countercyclical pattern (see for example Bentolila and Jimeno 2006). We would accordingly expect these two variables to be inversely related. Basically, one can always come up with some sensible economic explanations through which a two-way relationship between them is established. But as we are interested in identifying causality toward unemployment, our efforts are nevertheless aimed at pinpointing theoretical channels whereby labour productivity influences unemployment. Economic theory posits that there are two basic avenues which could explain this influence: (i) given an output level, a decline in labour productivity growth leads to a rise in demand for labour that, for a fixed labour supply, would cause unemployment to decrease, and (ii) when labour productivity goes up, for a given wage level, unit labour costs drop, which renders firms' products more competitive and boosts employment.

[5] However, in Blanchard and Wolfers (2000) shocks to TFP growth are treated as having permanent effects on unemployment. These authors present econometric evidence that a 1 % drop in the underlying TFP growth rate prompts a 0.73 % increase in unemployment. Nickell's (1997) approach to the effects of TFP growth on unemployment, on the other hand, differs from Blanchard and Wolfers' (2000) in that they are taken to be only temporary. According to his findings, a 1 % reduction in TFP growth gives rise to a 0.86 % increase in unemployment. By contrast, no effects are found by Bertola et al. (2001).

Finally, the unemployment rate is also Granger-caused by the Capital Stock available (as a proportion of GDP) and by the resources that the economy devotes to accumulating this capital, captured by GFCF (as a percentage of GDP). Both variables turn out to be significant, the former at 5 % and the latter at 1 %. Economic booms often lead to high investment rates, and hence to a greater capital stock over time, which usually triggers a higher demand for labour, thereby increasing employment. Another potential channel of influence could be the following: assuming that workers and firms lack perfect information, a slowdown in TFP growth would temporarily raise unit labour costs and therefore would depress profit rates, thereby inducing firms to devote fewer resources to investment projects and hence to hire fewer workers (e.g. Blanchard 1998).

3.2.2 *Open Economy, Fiscal and Monetary Variables*

When we turn to the open economy side, three different variables are observed to have an effect on the unemployment rate: the Current Account Balance (as a percentage of GDP), NIIP, and the proportion of GDP which is accounted for by international trade (exports plus imports of goods and services). One of the reasons agreed upon by most analysts worldwide whereby the Great Recession came about is the so-called global imbalances, that is to say, the fact that some countries, mainly industrialised ones, such as the United States, Spain, Portugal, Greece, the U.K. or Australia, to name a few, were allowed to run huge current account deficits and to pile up an overwhelming amount of external debt because many others were willing to finance them by running current account surpluses of similar magnitude, these being primarily China, oil exporting countries and Germany (see for example Obstfeld and Rogoff 2009). Blanchard and Milesi-Ferretti (2012) address the issue of whether it is desirable from an economic viewpoint that current account deficits be reduced. The correct response to this question hinges on whether the deficit arises due to "good" or "bad" reasons. Regardless of what these reasons are, changes in the current account and increases in net foreign liabilities should have an influence over the economic activity and hence over the unemployment rate (see the recent work of Catão and Milesi-Ferretti 2013, where they largely succeed in "predicting" past crises both in advanced and developing economies by thoroughly analysing the ratio of net foreign liabilities to GDP, and in particular its net external debt component). Against this background, it comes as no surprise to see the first two variables Granger-causing the Spanish unemployment rate.

Concerning the relationship between openness to trade and unemployment, we find Granger-causality at 10 % of significance. While international trade is usually seen by laymen as having deleterious effects on unemployment, academic analyses tend to yield more ambiguous results. Some economists assert that trade and unemployment are not related (see for example Krugman 1993; Attanasio et al. 2004, the latter failing to trace an empirical link between trade and the likelihood of unemployment). Others carry out theoretical and empirical studies that show otherwise. To cite but a couple of examples, Brecher (1974) and Davis (1998) both use an augmented Heckscher–Ohlin model with minimum wages whereby trade liberalization can increase unemployment. By relying on Melitz (2003)-type models –with heterogeneous firms–, another strand of the literature seeks to shed some light on this potential relationship. Some of them combine this kind of models with search frictions in the labour market and come to the conclusion that an unemployment hike would be likely to occur in the aftermath of a process of trade liberalization (or of tariff reduction). This increase would arise because job destruction in small firms would exceed job creation in large ones (see for example Janiak 2006). However, as a downside, this framework does not succeed in accounting for the inter-sectoral labour reallocation flows that we see in practice when an economy opens up to trade. Other authors –see for example Makioka (2011)–, by including an additional perfect-competitive homogeneous sector into the aforementioned models, find conflicting effects on unemployment that may cancel out: international trade creates jobs in the monopolistically competitive sector and this job creation leads to labour market tightness, which induces some workers to move into the dynamic sector. Helpman and Itskhoki (2010) also follow the same approach and find that globalization can push unemployment up. Finally, Menezes-Filho and Muendler (2011) find that the Brazilian workers displaced by tariff cuts are not completely absorbed by those expanding exporter sectors, thereby resulting in higher average unemployment.

On the fiscal front, we find Public Spending, Total and Tax Revenue, Public Deficit and Debt to have an impact on the common factor; indeed not a surprising result, given what economic theory dictates about the effects of government stimuli on short-run economic activity. This is a much-debated economic topic central to the issue of fiscal consolidation currently at work in most European Union countries and elsewhere. There has certainly been in the recent past some controversy among economists over whether fiscal adjustments have expansionary or contractionary effects on short-run economic activity. The Great Recession and the restrictive policies that ensued from it seem to have settled this dispute in favour of the Keynesian branch (for a recent work making a case for the greater effectiveness of big fiscal stimuli in liquidity trap situations, see for example Delong and Summers, 2012). Going into a more in-depth analysis, as Ilzetzki et al. (2013) uncover, the effectiveness of fiscal policy in boosting output and employment very much relies on four insights or features: (i) whether the economy in question is a developed or a developing country. For the latter, the response of output (and employment) to public spending increases is lower and less persistent than in the former case; (ii) whether the country operates under a fixed or flexible exchange rate. In the former case, the fiscal multiplier effect will be much larger than if the currency is allowed to freely fluctuate in the market; (iii) whether the country is relatively closed or open. The more closed it is, the bigger the fiscal impact on output and employment will be; and (iv) whether the debt-to-GDP ratio is high or low. The higher it is, the lower and shorter-lived the effect of fiscal expansions will be. This being said, by and large most economists now think of short-term expansionary fiscal retrenchments as particular episodes in which these effects are made possible due to the conjunction of several factors. The disagreement nowadays appears to centre on the size of fiscal multipliers, with some economists like Barro arguing that fiscal multipliers in peacetimes are essentially zero, and with others like Krugman and Romer advocating a big stimulus package to get the US economy back on track.[6]

As regards monetary variables, we just come across one that anticipates a change in the common factor: (nominal) Money Supply (M3), found significant at 5 %. We can interpret this causal relationship as occurring only in the short-run, although there is a fertile strand of the literature that deals with the long-lasting effects of monetary policy on unemployment (see for example Ball 2009). In a context of price rigidity, monetary shocks bring about changes in real variables, such as output and unemployment, through the real interest rate and real exchange rate avenues, regardless of the time span allowed for. However, prices tend to fully adjust in the medium to long-run, rendering monetary policy shocks ineffective when it comes to spurring or cooling down the economy. However, as Blanchard (2003) argues, even if the VAR literature suggests that the monetary policy effects are largely gone after 2–3 years, in practice there may be a longer way to get to the long-run. Admittedly, even recognising the constraints we face owing to the methodology employed, we do not completely succeed in providing a full account of these effects since the different measures of real interest rate and real exchange rate are not found significant in Granger-causing the unemployment rate.

3.2.3 Labour Variables

As far as the group of labour variables is concerned, Employment and Inactivity Rates are found to be relevant variables in accounting for changes in the unemployment rate. It is certainly a familiar fact that the Spanish economy has always suffered from a high inactivity rate (see Blanchard and Jimeno 1995), and increasing it has long been prescribed as key to having a more dynamic labour market.

It is worth pausing for a moment to mention what we see as a rather striking fact: the absence of Long-term Unemployment (over Total Unemployment) within the group of significant variables. We would have expected this variable to have been important in explaining the Spanish (core) unemployment rate. Over the past three decades Spanish and foreign macroeconomists and labour economists have

[6] International Monetary Fund (IMF) economists have devoted considerable effort to analysing this burning issue. For example, Blanchard and Leigh (2013) contend that the short-run fiscal multipliers should be neither the only nor the most important aspect within the fiscal adjustment strategy. A good decision would involve pondering over the benefits derived from and the pain inflicted on the economy by cutting government outlays today and would compare them to the positive and negative effects of the alternative "wait today and do later" on output and employment. The strength of the private sector would drive the optimal fiscal strategy in each economy.

strived to comprehend the mechanisms through which long-term unemployment builds up and whereby it hinders the performance of the labour market.

A generous and poorly designed unemployment benefit system, coupled with an industry-level wage bargaining arrangement in which insiders pursue their own interests when setting wages, has inevitably given rise to the development of this phenomenon in some European countries (Nickell et al. 2005), Spain being one of the countries in which it has gathered most importance. As for its consequences, the long-term unemployment trap has proven to be harmful for the well-functioning of the labour market, as it weakens the link between unemployment and wages (see Jimeno and Bentolila 1998). Indeed, the dissuasive effects that a rising unemployment has on wages can vanish if long-term unemployment largely accounts for this increase, thereby preventing the self-correcting mechanism in the labour market from working properly.[7]

Another variable on which we place our focus is the Labour Market Tightness (LMT), defined as the number of vacancies divided by the number of unemployed people. As it is widely known in the literature –see for example Pissarides (2000)–, this concept turns out to be essential to explaining what the probability of a vacancy being filled with an unemployed or a worker is, so that when the LMT is high, firms find it hard to fill a vacancy because nearly everyone is employed and there are many vacancies unfilled in the market. On the contrary, if it is low, vacancies can be filled quite quickly since many candidates are willing to exit unemployment and get a job. This variable is also deemed to be important in explaining labour mobility and other facts (Shimer 2010).[8] Our analysis points to the result of the common factor being Granger-caused by the LMT at the 1 % significance level.

To conclude with this group, we address variables such as the percentage of workers classified by range of age or by the economic sector in which they are employed (in both cases expressed in percentage terms relative to total workers). Regarding the first classification, our analysis seems to yield coherent results, indicating that those age segments of workers whose possibilities of entering the labour market are scantiest, namely young people (Workers aged 16–24) –see Dolado et al. (2000)–, Granger-cause the common factor, with a significance level of 10 %. As for the second classification, we obtain interesting results as well, as Construction Sector and Services Sector Workers –along with Agricultural Sector Workers– are found to Granger-cause the unemployment rate, both at 1 %. The former variable refers to an economic sector in Spain whose importance in explaining the last economic crisis is hard to overstate.[9] As regards the latter

[7] This lack of adjustment associated with the role of long-term unemployment is likely to have been compensated for by the effect of the flexibility reforms undertaken in recent times.

[8] For an analysis of Spanish vacancies and unemployed workers in terms of matching, see Álvarez de Toledo et al. (2008, 2011, 2013).

[9] We will again touch upon the relationship between the construction sector and unemployment in the group of price variables by looking at housing prices and their significance in Granger-causing the latter variable.

variable, the tertiary sector has long been and is currently the main driver of the Spanish economy, accounting for roughly 70 % of the total economic activity and employment.

3.2.4 Labour Cost Variables

We now move on to the next group of variables, those fitting into the general concept of labour cost. Within this common label, we find several variables that have an effect on the unemployment rate. For clarity of exposition, they are split into three different subcategories: Unit Labour Cost (ULC), Wage Cost (in nominal terms), and Minimum Wages. Two variables pertaining to the first subgroup are found significant in explaining the unemployment rate: ULC Index and ULC growth, both from OECD databases. The first variable is an index constructed by the OECD intended to gauge international competitiveness. Economic booms usually give rise to increases in ULC insofar as upward pressure on wage growth in excess of labour productivity growth strongly arises. The converse is expected to occur in recessions. This tendency is even exacerbated in the Spanish economy, since, as stressed earlier, labour productivity behaves in a countercyclical fashion – via massive creation/destruction of temporary employment. These ULC increases (decreases) lead to real appreciations (depreciations), which in turn bring about losses (gains) in employment. Spain, since before the advent of democracy, has undergone these pronounced ups and downs of competitiveness, although it is worth underscoring that significant downward wage corrections have proven hard to materialise (Jimeno and Bentolila 1998), the Great Recession being perhaps the exception. As expected, we find in our analysis both variables, ULC index and ULC growth, to Granger-cause the common factor at 5 and 1 % level of significance, respectively.

With respect to the second subgroup, which focuses on a fundamental labour variable, the price of labour, we come up with two statistically significant variables: Total Wage Cost and Mean Wage. The first concept refers to the monthly wage payment –Ordinary Wage Cost– plus extraordinary and delayed payments. The second variable needs no further explanation. By means of a standard New Keynesian model with staggered wage setting applied to the U.S. economy from the mid-1980s onwards, Galí (2011) demonstrates that wage inflation and unemployment are negatively correlated over those periods when price inflation is low and stable. This theoretical result is confirmed by simple Granger-causality tests indicating that wage inflation Granger-causes unemployment. For references covering the Spanish case, something has already been said throughout the present work about the link between wage movements and unemployment in Spain, to which parts we refer the reader, who is also encouraged to consult the abundant literature on this issue—see, for instance, Bentolila and Dolado (1994) and Jimeno and Bentolila (1998).

On the third subgroup, minimum wages are regarded to be one of the main labour institutions prevailing in most industrialised and emerging markets, so perhaps a more convenient place to address this variable would have been within the eighth group ("institutional variables"). However, our decision has been to include it into the labour cost group for the sake of uniformity. One is the measure of the minimum wage that Granger-causes the unemployment rate: Ratio of Minimum Wage to Mean Wage, taken from the FRDB-IMF Labour Institutions Database. This variable is found significant at 1 %. In principle, according to a perfectly competitive model, a minimum wage set above the market-clearing wage unequivocally reduces employment compared to the outcome in a minimum wage-free situation. However, if this institution is introduced into an imperfectly competitive labour market, there is a theoretical possibility for a minimum wage to increase employment (see for example Stigler 1946). This positive relationship may also be theoretically possible if a dual labour market exists and the minimum wage is not binding in the informal market. To sum up, empirical evidence about this issue points to either direction: the effect of a minimum wage on employment can either be positive or negative—see for example Dolado et al. (1996) and Neumark et al. (2013).

3.2.5 Price Variables

That large housing price movements can be associated with the unemployment rate is textbook economics. Picture a situation where a housing bubble arises with the help of foreign capital pouring into the country. Unemployment is expected to come down as aggregate demand expands. Once foreign capital inflows dry up and the bubble bursts, aggregate demand will plummet and unemployment will soar, which is likely to push the financial system into going bust, thereby further contributing to increasing the unemployment rate. Our Granger-causality results support this story by suggesting that the variable Housing Prices leads the unemployment rate. This same outcome is found in Antipa and Lecat (2010), where these authors present a structural model of the demand and supply sides of the housing market with an error-correction process through which they intend to assess whether this price behaviour in France and Spain can be wholly accounted for by bubbles or alternatively it is demographic and financial factors that can account for the price dynamics observed. They conclude that their analysis points to fundamentals being the relevant factors in explaining the housing price dynamics seen in both countries, although they do not preclude departures from equilibrium prices due to loose credit conditions. Also, in line with our results, Álvarez and Cabrero (2010) state that housing prices series have proven a useful tool for predicting future output (neither past nor contemporaneous one).

What happens to the unemployment rate when an oil or energy price shock arises? Our simple analysis does not yield a quantitative outcome but it enables us to assess whether the latter impacts on the former variable. Three energy price measures are found to Granger-cause the common factor: Oil Price, in US dollars and in Euros, and Energy Price Index; the first and the last one at 1 %, and the second one at 5 %. At first glance, the direct relationship between oil (or energy) price changes and employment in an oil-importer country like Spain seems crystal clear (Caraballo and Usabiaga 2009). On the one hand, higher oil prices entail fewer resources available to be spent on other uses, so we should expect oil price spikes to take a toll on unemployment as retail business would suffer and start laying workers off. On the other hand, more expensive crude oil often raises production and transport costs, which in turn leads output to shrink and employment to decrease. But unfortunately, things are not that simple. When this rise is brought about by an economic boom, the previous negative effect on employment may be offset by the greater aggregate demand. So the net outcome is ambiguous.

Expectations also play an important role here. If the oil price shock is not perceived as permanent by economic agents, firms will not risk firing workers as they would rather pursue a labour-hoarding strategy. The squeeze on profits will be taken to be temporary and firms will hold on until prices return to normal. Thus, the connection between oil prices swings and the unemployment rate then vanishes. In addition, the aforementioned profit squeeze might be dampened if wages did not react much to the oil price spike. Against this backdrop, coordinated collective bargaining systems usually lead to better outcomes concerning unemployment than do more decentralised ones. Finally, if the more realistic assumption that the central bank follows a monetary rule is thrown in, a shock to the price of oil should trigger a change in the monetary policy stance that may end up having some impact on the unemployment rate.

In order to get a sense of the effects of an oil price hike on employment (or on the unemployment rate), it is convenient to look into the existing empirical literature. Blanchard and Galí (2007) assess different potential causes whereby recent oil shocks have not been as disturbing to developed economies as they were back in the early 1970s and 1980s and highlight four as the main ones: good circumstances, small share of oil in production, more flexible labour markets, and a more efficient monetary policy. Blanchard and Riggi (2013), by building on the latter article, claim that the fading correlation between oil shocks and business cycles for the United States in recent times can be ascribed firstly to a lower real wage rigidity spurred by weaker unions, increasing competition in product markets and a declining minimum wage, and secondly to a more credible monetary policy which has done a good job at anchoring inflation expectations.[10]

[10] Many other authors (Nordhaus 2007; Kilian 2008; Blinder and Rudd 2012) second this view of the weakening association between oil price increases and declines in economic activity over the last two decades and add some other reasons that could account for this finding. An exception is Hamilton (2009), who argues that an oil price hike seems to have decisively contributed to transforming an economic slowdown into the Great Recession.

3.2.6 Institutional Variables

In turning to the group of institutional variables, we are faced with seven important variables that Granger-cause the unemployment rate: Employment Protection Legislation (EPL), Union Coverage, ALMPs, Human Capital, Urban Population (as a percentage of Total Population), Gross Unemployment Benefit Replacement Rate (two-year average) and Benefit Duration Index. They all are significant at 1 %, except for Union Coverage, whose statistical significance is 10 %, and Urban Population, significant at 5 %.

The first variable is considered to be one of the main ingredients of "Eurosclerosis". The economic literature on the effect of EPL on the unemployment rate is quite extensive (Layard et al. 1991; Nickell et al. 2005). EPL refers to the imposition of legal constraints on dismissals and of compensations to workers that employers willing to terminate a labour contract must face. From a theoretical viewpoint, a strict EPL is believed to reduce both flows from and into employment –that is, separation and hiring rates– by raising legal barriers to dismissing workers and by making employers more cautious about hiring. In other words, a stringent EPL involves an inflexible labour market in which the necessary adjustments for a well-functioning economy (for resources to reallocate from low-productivity to high-productivity industries) may take longer than normal, with a negative effect on the productivity evolution (Burgess 1994). It should be mentioned that this adverse scenario might be a close fit to the Spanish case.

The article by Bentolila and Bertola (1990) represents one of the seminal studies about the EPL's effects on employment. By laying out a dynamic partial equilibrium model with uncertainty, they show that high firing (and hiring) costs slightly lead to a greater average employment level both in bad times and in the long-run. But they caution that when a more complete model with endogenous firm creation and destruction is used, the aforesaid conclusion should be qualified: the net effect of a non-marginal reduction of the EPL on the overall level of employment is likely to be ambiguous since it gives employers more incentives to both hire and fire workers.[11]

Within those who think of employment protection laws as being neutral to the unemployment rates, we can mention Blanchard and Portugal (2001). In effect, in their article they compared the US, one of the countries in the world with the lowest EPL, with Portugal, one of the countries with the strictest legislation. What they observed is that, despite this huge difference in EPL, the unemployment rate in both countries was roughly the same about a decade ago. This is accounted for by asserting that EPL is expected to influence two labour variables at the same time, whose effects on the unemployment rate run counter to each other and are likely to be offset, rendering the unemployment rate unchanged. Indeed, a strict EPL reduces job flows from employment to unemployment, as firms would be

[11] As stated below, more time is needed in order to compute the effect of the recent Spanish reforms regarding EPL over the entire business cycle.

induced to fire less, thereby leading to a lower unemployment rate, and it would also increase unemployment duration, which would make unemployment higher.

Another way through which a stringent EPL might affect unemployment and give rise to lack of adjustment in the labour market is by enabling workers who already have jobs (the insiders) to bargain or advocate for wage increases above those that would be compatible with a better overall employment outcome. Indeed, these wage rises, by being detached from those grounded on economic fundamentals, would stop the unemployed (the outsiders) from finding jobs and could even cast them into long-term unemployment in the presence of hysteresis mechanisms (Blanchard and Summers 1986, 1987).

With respect to the Spanish case, Bentolila et al. (2012) expand the original insider–outsider model to include temporary workers and label it as two-tier or dual labour market. These temporary workers can be thought of as outsiders in that they almost lack employment protection, they are subjected to high turnover rates as the bulk of the adjustment when good times turn bad falls on them, and accordingly barely have influence over the wage setting process. On this basis, a compelling comparison between the Spanish and French labour markets is carried out. With similar labour market institutions, the surge of the unemployment rate in both countries throughout the Great Recession has been very dissimilar. In the second quarter of 2013, France had an unemployment rate of 10.9, whereas Spain's was 26.2. The authors settle this puzzle by underlining two main differences between the Spanish and French EPLs, which combined, can account for a considerable bulk of the differential increase in Spanish unemployment: (i) the gap between permanent and temporary workers' firing costs is much wider in Spain, and (ii) the regulation of fixed-term contracts is much stricter in France, impairing a free use of them. The main contribution of the paper is that the authors calibrate a theoretical model so as to compute what the rise in the Spanish unemployment rate would have been had the EPL features been that of the French labour market. They find that there would have been a rise of 4.1 % points in the Spanish unemployment rate rather than the 7.5 % point increase observed between 2005–2007 and 2008–2009.[12]

The second institutional variable shown to be jointly significant –at 10 %– in Granger-causing the common factor is the Union Coverage (UC) or Collective Bargaining Coverage, the proportion of workers covered by collective agreements. From a theoretical viewpoint, establishing a relationship between UC and

[12] A new strand of the literature takes a step further and links the EPL to the Central Bank's monetary policy stance (Faia et al. 2013). These authors claim that firing costs matter for the efficiency of monetary policy and make a case for it to be targeted at lowering the productivity-reducing externalities triggered by high firing costs. When applied to the European Monetary Union, the policy implications are for the heterogeneous firing costs across countries to be harmonised so that the efficiency of the single monetary policy is enhanced. Besides, even though our main interest lies in explaining the relationship between EPL and aggregate unemployment (or employment), it should be noted that EPL is likely to have important effects on the unemployment rate of different groups of workers. Recent empirical evidence suggests that less skilled workers are hurt the most by strict EPLs (MacLeod and Nakavachara 2007).

aggregate employment (or unemployment) does not prove hard. By using a straightforward model with only two sectors, one in which all firms are unionised and where all jobs are assumed to be good, and a secondary (competitive) sector of manual (unskilled) workers, Layard et al. (1991) show that an increase in UC raises unionised employment, which in turn means that total employment rises as well, provided that the labour supply to the competitive sector is not very elastic. If this latter assumption is not met, it follows that aggregate employment will contract. The same authors provide empirical evidence as to how much this institutional variable manages to account for cross-section differences in the unemployment rates observed over the period 1983–1988. They find a positive relationship between coverage of collective bargaining and the unemployment rate: a high UC harms employment, although the reverse occurs if the bargaining is highly coordinated.

Following up on his joint work with Layard and Jackman, Nickell (1997) finds that an increase by one unit in the union coverage index would bid up the unemployment rate in 3.6 % points and that a rise of one unit in the bargaining coordination index would reduce the unemployment rate in 3.7 % points. Similarly, Fitoussi et al. (2000) make use of a model that features the interaction of shocks and institutions (in the same spirit of that of Blanchard and Wolfers 2000) and find that UC and bargaining coordination are positive and negatively related to unemployment, respectively.[13]

A measure that has recurrently been cited in academic and political circles as one of the most powerful remedies for curing the Spanish unemployment disease is to spend more (and of course more efficiently) on ALMPs. Many national and international economists, as well as other analysts working in international organisations, prescribe an increasing amount of resources devoted to these policies as a way to overcome market failures stemming from a relatively generous welfare state, and especially the long-term unemployment predicament. This policy is known to be one of the main pillars that make up a more general strategy dubbed "flexicurity" –essentially, a combination of Anglo-Saxon labour market flexibility and Continental Europe's security for workers–,[14] as was made popular in Denmark back in the 1990s. It is widely known that the so-called Mediterranean countries have a lot of room for improvement when it comes to enhancing ALMPs

---

[13] By the same token, Baker et al. (2005) display results that are in line with Nickell (1997) and Fitoussi et al. (2000): UC leads to higher unemployment, although it is worth emphasising that this result is only significant at 10 %. They also obtain the same outcome as the previous aforesaid articles concerning the effects of bargaining coordination on the unemployment rate. On the other hand, in Nunziata (2003) it is reported that UC has a significant detrimental impact on employment growth only during economic expansions. Other studies have also tackled this empirical relationship between UC and unemployment without much success. An example of these is Jimeno and Rodríguez-Palenzuela (2003), where the coefficient associated with aggregate unemployment is not statistically significant, although when gender differences are introduced, female unemployment is observed to be affected by UC.

[14] Low layoff costs in exchange for a generous unemployment benefit system and intense ALMPs.

since they tend to allocate few resources to this area when compared with the Nordic countries, for example.

According to Boeri and van Ours (2008), four different kinds of ALPMs can be identified: (i) training for unemployed and employed adults at peril of losing their jobs, (ii) subsidised employment, targeted at those priority groups, (iii) public employment services, such as job search courses, administration of unemployment benefits, etc., and (iv) activation, which refers to measures associated with the general term "stick": incentives for job seekers to intensify the search process, such as sanctions or compulsory participation in training programs or subsidised employment.

Economic theory asserts that ALMPs may improve the efficiency of the labour market, which amounts to an inward shift of the Beveridge curve –see Álvarez de Toledo et al. (2013) for Spain. That is, given a vacancy rate, the unemployment rate will drop. Boone and van Ours (2004) set up a model in which ALMPs can curtail unemployment. This would come about through two different channels: (i) the job-finding rate may rise, although this theoretical effect is regarded as ambiguous, (ii) a better trained worker can land better paid jobs (and with lower job destruction rates). In this regard, training is considered to reduce unemployment, whereas subsidised jobs and public employment services are believed to be not as effective in bringing it down.[15]

Our econometric analysis also reports that the variable Human Capital Granger-causes the unemployment rate at the 1 % level of significance. Investment in human capital is usually related to unemployment through the concept of skilled-biased technical change. As Violante (2008) puts it, "skill-biased technical change is a shift in the production technology that favours skilled over unskilled labour by increasing its relative productivity and, therefore, its relative demand." Therefore, as this process goes on, unskilled workers will find themselves losing their jobs or not being able to get a new one. It follows that raising spending on education and training, by providing a greater proportion of the population with that indispensable set of skills for finding qualified jobs, should contribute to cutting unemployment. In accordance with this view and with the common shocks-institutions interactions approach, Krugman (1994) raises the issue of both the increases in European unemployment and in income inequality in Anglo-Saxon countries as being two sides of the same coin. Thus, the emergence of a technological shift biased toward skill-intensive innovation led to a fall in the relative demand for unskilled labour, which, in the presence of employment-unfriendly labour market institutions in

[15] In reviewing what empirical evidence says about the relationship between ALMPs and unemployment, we are also confronted with opposite results. On the one hand, Layard et al. s' (1991) regressions imply the existence of a negative relationship between these variables. Nickell (1997) shows that a 10 % increase in ALMPs spending leads the unemployment rate to drop by 2.4 %. Likewise, Elmeskov et al. (1998) find that an increase of 10 % in ALMPs spending causes a 1.47 % reduction in the unemployment rate. On the other hand, Blanchard and Wolfers (2000), Bertola et al. (2001) and Jimeno and Rodríguez-Palenzuela (2003) fail to find a clear link between ALMPs and aggregate unemployment.

continental Europe, brought about an acute rise in unemployment, whereas in the U.S., on the contrary, this same shock gave rise to greater wage inequality, with no permanent rise in unemployment. This development was made possible by the larger downward wage flexibility in place in the American economy.

Looking down into a more disaggregated (regional) level, the percentage of people living in urban areas –Urban Population– may be thought to affect unemployment figures. This variable, following the general pattern of increasing urbanisation observed in Europe, has continually been rising in Spain since 1950, although at a slower pace from the early 1980s onwards. Given that in Spain wage flexibility and geographic mobility of labour have been lacking (Jimeno and Bentolila 1998), at least up until recently, the geographic distribution of the population may affect the aggregate unemployment rate.

The last two labour institutions considered are the existing measures available as time series that capture the generosity of unemployment benefits: Gross Unemployment Benefit Replacement Rate (2-year average) and Unemployment Benefit Duration Index. The former compares unemployment benefits received when unemployed to wages earned when employed. The greater the coverage is, the more generous the system will be. In principle, for a country suffering from mass unemployment, the usual advice would be to advocate cutting benefit replacement rates as a powerful incentive for the unemployed to intensify their job search and strive to abandon that lame situation.[16]

However, a deeper incursion into the topic in question will evidence that most labour economists and macroeconomists dealing with labour market issues tend to think of this institution individually considered as being less harmful to unemployment,[17] provided that the benefit does not last for too long and that an array of different incentives exists that pushes the unemployed toward active job search and toward acquiring skills through training courses (ALMPs). Denmark is a country often viewed as the benchmark in this regard. Back in the 1990s it went through a deep reform of the operation of its unemployment benefit system and nowadays manages to combine a high replacement rate, which falls short of those in place in other countries concerning the length of time over which they are available, with a high strictness with which the system is operated. That is to say, the criteria for benefit receipt have been tightened, and an extensive collection of sanctions has been implemented with the aim of accomplishing the enforcement of these criteria.

[16] Actually, in 2012, the Spanish Government reduced the replacement rate from 60 % of the net reference pay to 50 %, applicable from the 7th month following the first day on which the unemployed starts receiving the subsidy.

[17] Álvarez de Toledo et al. (2008, 2011) test, with macroeconomic and individual data from the Spanish public employment agencies respectively, the plausibility of the stock-flow model (Coles and Smith 1998) for the Spanish economy. In essence, they conclude that there exists clear evidence of this type of labour market segmentation. More specifically, the results point to an extreme case of that scheme: a queue of workers. In this scenario, the search intensity is almost fruitless without labour mobility.

In this work we are however concerned with the benefit replacement rate in isolation as a significant determinant of the unemployment rate. Our results point to the former variable as being relevant in explaining changes in the latter at a level of significance of 1 %. A quick broad-brush review of the existing (and by now familiar) literature covering this causal relationship confirms that the majority of these studies yields the same result. By drawing on their cross-section regressions for a sample of 20 countries over the period 1983–1988, Layard et al. (1991) take the stand that a rise in the benefit replacement rate leads to higher unemployment. Nickell (1997) derives the result that a 10 % point increase in the benefit replacement rate raises the unemployment rate by 0.88 %, whereas Blanchard and Wolfers (2000) obtain a 0.70 % figure. Elmeskov et al. (1998) and Nickell et al. (2002) evidence that a 10 % rise in the replacement rate would produce a 1.29 % and 1.24 % increase in the unemployment rate, respectively. However, the effect of a 10 % higher replacement rate on unemployment discovered by Belot and van Ours (2004) turns out to be small, 0.10 %, but significant.[18]

As already mentioned above, the unemployment benefit duration is thought to be closely related to the level of unemployment and specifically to long-term unemployment. Many empirical studies have found a tight relation between these two variables. Layard et al. (1991) derive a coefficient in the cross-sectional regression (with the unemployment rate as the dependent variable) of 0.92. Nickell (1997) and Nickell et al. (2002, 2005), on the other hand, find that increasing the benefit duration by one year leads to an unemployment rate rise of 0.70 and 0.17, respectively. Within those analyses that rely on interactions between macroeconomic shocks and labour institutions, Blanchard and Wolfers (2000) and Bertola et al. (2001) arrive at higher numbers: the former obtain 1.27 and the latter 1.43.

References

Álvarez LJ, Cabrero A (2010) Does housing really lead the business cycle? In: Bandt O, Knetsch T, Peñalosa J, Zollino F (eds) Housing markets in Europe. A macroeconomic perspective. Springer, Berlin, pp 61–84

Álvarez de Toledo P, Núñez F, Usabiaga C (2008) La Función de Emparejamiento y el Mercado de Trabajo Español. Revista de Economía Aplicada 16(48):5–35

Álvarez de Toledo P, Núñez F, Usabiaga C (2011) An empirical analysis of the matching process in Andalusian public employment agencies. Hacienda Pública Española 198(3):67–102

Álvarez de Toledo P, Núñez F, Usabiaga C (2013) An empirical approach on labour segmentation. Applications with individual duration data. Econ Model, forthcoming

Antipa P, Lecat R (2010) The "housing bubble" and financial factors: insights from a structural model of the French and Spanish residential markets. In: Bandt O, Knetsch T, Peñalosa J, Zollino F (eds) Housing markets in Europe. A macroeconomic perspective. Springer, Berlin, pp 161–186

---

[18] Baker et al. (2005)'s outcome contradicts those reported above. They make the point that if the government raises the replacement rate, unemployment will decline, as long as the benefit duration is not extended too much.

Attanasio O, Goldberg P, Pavcnik N (2004) Trade reforms and wage inequality in Colombia. J Dev Econ 74(2):331–366

Baker D, Glyn A, Howell DR, Schmitt J (2005) Labor market institutions and unemployment: a critical assessment of the cross-country evidence. In: Howell DR (ed) Fighting unemployment: the limits of free market orthodoxy. Oxford University Press, Oxford, pp 72–118

Ball L (2009) Hysteresis in unemployment: old and new evidence. National Bureau of Economic Research (NBER), Working Paper No. 14818

Ball L, Leigh D, Loungani P (2013) Okun's law: fit at fifty? National Bureau of Economic Research (NBER), Working Paper No. 18668

Belot M, van Ours J (2004) Does the recent success of some OECD countries in lowering their unemployment rate lie in the clever design of their economic reforms? Oxf Econ Pap 56(4):621–642

Bentolila S, Bertola G (1990) Firing costs and labour demand: how bad is Eurosclerosis? Rev Econ Stud 57(3):381–402

Bentolila S, Dolado JJ (1994) Labour flexibility and wages: lessons from Spain. Econ Policy 9(18):55–99

Bentolila S, Jimeno JF (2006) Spanish unemployment: the end of the wild ride? In: Werding M (ed) Structural unemployment in Western Europe: reasons and remedies. MIT Press, Cambridge, pp 317–344

Bentolila S, Cahuc P, Dolado JJ, Le Barbanchon T (2012) Two-tier labour markets in the great recession: France versus Spain. Econ J 122(562):F155–F187

Bertola G, Blau FD, Kahn LM (2001) Comparative analysis of labor market outcomes: lessons for the United States from international long-run evidence. In: Krueger AB, Solow R (eds) The roaring nineties: can full employment be sustained?. Russell Sage Foundation, New York, pp 159–218

Blanchard OJ (1998) Revisiting European unemployment: unemployment, capital accumulation, and factor prices. Geary Lecture, Economic and Social Research Institute

Blanchard OJ (2000) The economics of unemployment. Shocks, institutions, and interactions. Lionel Robbins Lecture, London School of Economics

Blanchard OJ (2003) Monetary policy and unemployment. Conference monetary policy and the labor market, in Honor of James Tobin, New School.

Blanchard OJ, Jimeno JF (eds) (1995) Unemployment in Spain: is there a solution? Centre for Economic Policy Research (CEPR), London

Blanchard OJ, Leigh D (2013) Growth forecast errors and fiscal multipliers. National Bureau of Economic Research (NBER), Working Paper No. 18779

Blanchard OJ, Milesi-Ferretti GL (2012) (Why) should current account balances be reduced? IMF Econ Rev 60(1):139–150

Blanchard OJ, Portugal P (2001) What hides behind an unemployment rate: comparing Portuguese and U.S. labor markets. Am Econ Rev 91(1):187–207

Blanchard OJ, Riggi M (2013) Why are the 2000s so different from the 1970s? A structural interpretation of changes in the macroeconomic effects of oil prices. J Eur Econ Assoc 11(5):1032–1052

Blanchard OJ, Summers LH (1986) Hysteresis and the European unemployment problem. NBER Macroecon Ann 1:15–78

Blanchard OJ, Summers LH (1987) Hysteresis in unemployment. Eur Econ Rev 31(1–2):288–295

Blanchard OJ, Wolfers J (2000) The role of shocks and institutions in the rise of European unemployment: the aggregate evidence. Econ J 110(462):1–33

Blanchard OJ, Solow R, Wilson BA (1995) Productivity and unemployment. Massachusetts Institute of Technology (MIT), Mimeo

Blinder AS, Rudd J (2012) The supply-shock explanation of the great stagflation revisited. In: The great inflation: the rebirth of modern central banking. National Bureau of Economic Research (NBER), pp 119–175

Boeri T, van Ours J (2008) The economics of imperfect labor markets. Princeton University Press, Princeton

Boone J, van Ours J (2004) Effective active labor market policies. Institute for the Study of Labor (IZA), Discussion Paper No. 1335
Brecher R (1974) Minimum wage rates and the pure theory of international trade. Q J Econ 88(1):98–116
Burgess S (1994) The reallocation of employment and the role of employment protection legislation. Centre for Economic Performance (CEP), London School of Economics (LSE), Discussion Paper No. 193
Caraballo MA, Usabiaga C (2009) The relevance of supply shocks for inflation: the Spanish case. Appl Econ 41(6):753–764
Catão L, Milesi-Ferretti G (2013) External liabilities and crises. International Monetary Fund (IMF), Working Paper No. 13/113
Coles MG, Smith E (1998) Marketplaces and matching. Int Econ Rev 39(1):239–254
Crespo-Cuaresma J (2003) Okun's law revisited. Oxf Bull Econ Stat 65(4):439–451
Davis D (1998) Does European unemployment prop up American wages? National labour markets and global trade. Am Econ Rev 88(3):478–494
DeLong JB, Summers L (2012) Fiscal policy in a depressed economy. Brookings Pap Econ Act, Spring:233–297
Dickey DA, Fuller WA (1979) Distribution of the estimators for autoregressive time series with a unit root. J Am Stat Assoc 74(366):427–431
Dolado JJ, Kramarz F, Machin S, Manning A, Margolis D, Teulings C, Saint-Paul G, Keen M (1996) The economic impact of minimum wages in Europe. Econ Policy 11(23):317–372
Dolado JJ, Felgueroso F, Jimeno JF (2000) Explaining youth labor market problems in Spain: Crowding-out, institutions, or technology shifts? Eur Econ Rev 44(4–6):943–956
Dolado JJ, García-Serrano C, Jimeno JF (2002) Drawing lessons from the boom of temporary jobs in Spain. Econ J 112(480):270–295
Elliot G, Rothenberg TJ, Stock JH (1996) Efficient tests for an autoregressive unit root. Econometrica 64(4):813–836
Elmeskov J, Martin J, Scarpetta S (1998) Key lessons for labour market reforms: evidence from OECD countries experience. Swed Econ Policy Rev 5(2):205–252
Faia E, Lechthaler W, Merkl C (2013) Labor selection, turnover costs and optimal monetary policy. J Money Credit Banking, forthcoming.
Fitoussi JP, Jestaz D, Phelps ES, Zoega G (2000) Roots of the recent recoveries: labor reforms or private sector forces? Brookings Pap Econ Act 31(1):237–311
Galí J (2011) The return of the Wage Phillips curve. J Eur Econ Assoc 9(3):436–461
Galí J, Rabanal P (2004) Technology shocks and aggregate fluctuations: how well does the RBC model fit postwar U.S. data? National Bureau of Economic Research (NBER), Working Paper No. 10636
García-Cintado AC, Usabiaga C (2013) La Ley de Okun Española y la Lenta Salida de la Crisis Laboral. Documentación Social, forthcoming
Hamilton JD (2009) Causes and consequences of the oil shock of 2007–08. Brookings Pap Econ Act, Spring:215–259
Helpman E, Itskhoki O (2010) Labour market rigidities, trade and unemployment. Rev Econ Stud 77(3):1100–1137
Ilzetzki E, Mendoza EG, Végh CA (2013) How big (small?) are fiscal multipliers? J Monetary Econ 60(2):239–254
Janiak A (2006) Does trade liberalization lead to unemployment? Theory and some evidence. ECARES-Université Libre de Bruxelles, Mimeo
Jimeno JF, Bentolila S (1998) Regional unemployment persistence (Spain, 1976–1994). Labour Econ 5(1):25–51
Jimeno JF, Rodríguez-Palenzuela D (2003) Youth unemployment in the OECD: demographic shifts, labour market institutions and macroeconomic shocks. European Network of Economic Policy Research Institute, Economics Working Paper No. 019
Kilian L (2008) The economic effects of energy price shocks. J Econ Lit 46(4):871–909

Krugman P (1993) What do undergraduates need to know about trade? Am Econ Rev 83(2):23–26

Krugman P (1994) Past and prospective causes of high unemployment. Econ Rev, Federal Reserve Bank of Kansas City, Q IV, 23–43

Layard R, Nickell S, Jackman R (1991) Unemployment. Macroeconomic performance and the labour market. Oxford University Press, Oxford

MacLeod B, Nakavachara V (2007) Can wrongful discharge law enhance employment? Econ J 117(521):218–278

Makioka R (2011) Trade, unemployment, and reallocation with search frictions. Hitotsubashi University, Mimeo

Melitz M (2003) The impact of trade on intraindustry reallocations and aggregate industry productivity. Econometrica 71(6):1695–1725

Menezes-Filho NA, Muendler MA (2011) Labor reallocation in response to trade reform. National Bureau of Economic Research (NBER), Working Paper No. 17372

Neumark D, Ian Salas JM, Wascher W (2013) Revisiting the minimum wage-employment debate: throwing out the baby with the bathwater? National Bureau of Economic Research (NBER), Working Paper No. 18681

Ng S, Perron P (2001) Lag length selection and the construction of unit root tests with good size and power. Econometrica 69(6):1519–1554

Nickell S (1997) Unemployment and labor market rigidities: Europe vs. North America. J Econ Perspect 11(3):55–74

Nickell S, Nunziata L, Ochel W, Quitini G (2002) The Beveridge curve, unemployment and wages in the OECD from the 1960s to the 1990s. Centre for Economic Performance (CEP), London School of Economics (LSE), Discussion Paper No. 0502

Nickell S, Nunziata L, Ochel W (2005) Unemployment in the OECD since the 1960s. What do we know? Econ J 115(500):1–27

Nordhaus WD (2007) Who's afraid of a big bad oil shock? Brookings Pap Econ Act, Fall, 219–238

Nunziata L (2003) Labour market institutions and the cyclical dynamics of employment. Labour Econ 10(1):31–53

Obstfeld M, Rogoff K (2009) Global imbalances and the financial crisis: products of common causes. In: Proceedings of the Federal Reserve Bank of San Francisco-Asia economic policy conference, pp 131–172

Pissarides C (2000) Equilibrium unemployment theory, 2nd edn. MIT Press, Cambridge

Shimer R (2010) Labor markets and business cycles. Princeton University Press, Princeton

Stigler GJ (1946) The economics of minimum wage legislation. Am Econ Rev 36:358

Usabiaga C (2010) La Relación entre el Crecimiento, el Desempleo y el Empleo: El Caso Español. Cuadernos de Información Económica 214:83–88

Violante GL (2008) Skill-biased technical change. In: Durlauf SN, Blume LE (eds) The new Palgrave dictionary of economics, 2nd edn. Palgrave Macmillan, Basingstoke

Blanchard OJ, Galí J (2007) The macroeconomic effects of oil price shocks: why are the 2000s so different from the 1970s? In: International dimensions of monetary policy. National Bureau of Economic Research (NBER), pp 373–421

Chapter 4
Policy Considerations Drawn from Our Results

Abstract From the outset of the Spanish democracy up to the current crisis, the different Spanish governments have unsuccessfully tried to change the existing set of poor institutions. This fact, matched up with adverse shocks, has led to a high and persistent unemployment, especially in certain regions. From an economic policy perspective, such bad institutions call for policy measures aimed at improving labour market flexibility conditions which are thought to speed up the adjustment process in response to adverse shocks, thereby preventing upward shifts in unemployment from becoming permanent. Our Granger-causality analysis appears to confirm these claims, as many institutional variables (EPL, unions, unemployment benefits, minimum wage, labour cost pressure, mismatch, low productivity, insufficient ALMPs) explain well the evolution of the common factor driving regional unemployment.

Keywords Spanish labour market · Policy implications

In spite of its methodological simplicity, the preceding section can be thought of as a reinforcement of the consensus drawn from the large existing literature on the Spanish unemployment rate. In this regard, we reckon that our Granger-causality analysis could be interpreted as a brief "road book" aimed at attempting to contribute to the understanding of what the main determinants of the shamefully high Spanish unemployment rate are and how to bring it down. We therefore intend to put the insights derived in that section to use by offering a non-exhaustive collection of recipes for curing or at least alleviating the Spanish labour market disease. In order to accomplish this goal, we basically disregard variables included in groups 1–4 and 7, not because we think they are not important in explaining the Spanish unemployment rate, but because in many cases affecting those variables is primarily out of Spanish policy makers' reach: for example, monetary policy is decided in Frankfurt, public finances are strongly constrained by the need to put the fiscal house in order and, in the background, by the Stability and Growth Pact, the debt deleveraging process is mainly out of the control of the government, energy prices depend largely on international factors, etc. That is why we would rather concentrate on labour and institutional variables with a stronger link to

A. García-Cintado et al., *Spanish Regional Unemployment*, SpringerBriefs in Economics,
DOI: 10.1007/978-3-319-03686-1_4,

unemployment. We shall see how the variables that our empirical analysis emphasises as relevant ones closely fit into the main causes of the Spanish unemployment behaviour.

A feasible explanation to the highly persistent behaviour we observe in the Spanish regional unemployment series might have to do with the "Eurosclerosis" argument. As it becomes evident from a simple glance at the specialised literature, the Spanish economy stands out in international comparisons as having a very inflexible labour market—at least up until the 2010–2012 reforms. One work well worth looking into is Nickell (1997): he builds up five labour indicators, based on working hours, fixed-term contracts, employment protection, minimum wages and workers' rights to collective bargaining, for a bunch of European countries and for North America. He finds that Spain and Italy both have extremely rigid labour markets. Remarkably, these indices have not undergone substantial changes over time, not even after several labour reforms undertaken by the Spanish government (Usabiaga 2007). The crux of the matter might lie in the interaction between adverse shocks and institutions, as was made popular more than a decade ago (Blanchard and Wolfers 2000). Along these lines, Bentolila and Jimeno (2006) point out that Spain has been subject to similar shocks to other OECD countries, except for the case of labour demand shocks, which have proven to be more important in the former. Thus, the Spanish unemployment differential vis-à-vis similar countries – mainly European countries – would relate more to a problem of unemployment-prone institutions than to idiosyncratic shocks. Among the former, these authors emphasise in particular employment protection legislation, unemployment benefits and collective bargaining. At the same time, Dolado and Jimeno (1997), using an SVAR model akin to the one applied in other studies for the Spanish economy (Gómez and Usabiaga 2001) – an insider-outsider model under complete hysteresis–, conclude that the behaviour of the Spanish unemployment rate can be reasonably well accounted for by introducing a plausible combination of shocks, along with the existence of highly persistent propagation mechanisms that are at work due to the rigidities in the labour and goods and services markets.

Jimeno and Bentolila (1998), on the other hand, put the blame of the high persistence exhibited by the Spanish regional unemployment on the low elasticities of migration and labour participation to wages and unemployment, and on the high real wage rigidity—see also Bentolila and Dolado (1994) concerning wage rigidity, with insider-outsider considerations. Regional wages barely react to local labour conditions, more likely moving in response to changes in national factors, which points to signs of the "demonstration effect" in the wage bargain process—see Usabiaga (2004) and Bande et al. (2008). This fact is quite related to the traditional collective bargaining system in Spain (Bentolila et al. 2010), whose intermediate degree of centralisation suffices to be labelled as an unemployment-prone one (Calmfors and Driffill 1998).[1] Finally, Bande and Karanassou (2009)

---

[1] Jimeno and Thomas (2011), by means of a one-sector Mortensen-Pissarides model with firm-specific productivity shocks, calibrated with typical continental European data, point out that the

state that the dynamics of the regional unemployment rates in Spain can be captured through the chain reaction theory of unemployment, and more specifically, through the interaction of slow adjustment processes and spill-over effects.

In summary, from the outset of the Spanish democracy up to the current crisis, the different Spanish governments have unsuccessfully tried to change the existing set of poor institutions. This fact, matched up with adverse shocks, has led to a high and persistent unemployment, especially in certain regions. From an economic policy perspective, such bad institutions call for policy measures aimed at improving labour market flexibility conditions which are thought to speed up the adjustment process in response to adverse shocks, thereby preventing upward shifts in unemployment from becoming permanent.

As a result of the acute and protracted current economic crisis, several reforms, basically intended to induce an internal devaluation, have been implemented in Spain. Naturally, these reforms include measures targeted at the labour market (2010–2012)—see Bentolila et al. (2012b). In this regard, it would be interesting to figure out the effect of these reforms on the medium-term Spanish unemployment rate.[2] Essentially, they have partially helped reduce the gap in the severance pay between open-ended and fixed-term contracts,[3] have facilitated the objective dismissal on economic grounds, and have fostered company-based bargaining, as well as the possibility of resorting to opt-out clauses whereby the firm may detach its wages and other labour conditions from those bargained at a superior level – country, region or industry – if the economic situation the company is going through calls for that.[4]

(Footnote 1 continued)
company-level bargaining system yields better results than those accomplished via sectorial collective agreements, being the efficient opting out of sector-level agreements also a good alternative to it. The 2012 labour reform aims to prioritise the applicability of collective agreements at the company level, consequently pushing for a greater decentralisation. The small size of many Spanish firms may clearly hamper this process.

[2] The current (as of October 2013) Spanish Government reckons that the reforms have helped cushion the employment destruction and that they will foster employment once recovery sets in. On the contrary, unions rebut that these reforms facilitate lay-offs and deteriorate the quality of the new jobs generated.

[3] Roughly speaking, it is worth noting that, in essence, the dismissal cost on permanent contracts drops from 45 days' pay per year worked (with an upper limit of 42 months) to 33 (with an upper limit of 24 months). As regards redundancy for economic reasons, the dismissal cost remains in 20 (with an upper limit of 12 months). As for the fixed-term contract, the dismissal cost increases —gradually— by 4 days' pay per year worked (from 8 to 12). Thus, the severance payment gap between permanent and temporary contracts clearly tends to shrink. However, it should be mentioned that the debate over the introduction of the single open-ended labour contract still goes on.

[4] By and large, these recent labour reforms follow the policy recommendations emanating from the IMF analysts. See Blanchard et al. (2013) for a set of tailor-made structural measures for advanced countries and Jaumotte (2011) for an application to the Spanish economy in the same spirit.

Also, a great deal of internal flexibility has been introduced, at least in theory.[5] For example, a wide range of administrative authorisations that hindered entrepreneurial activity have been removed, the German model of working hours has been partially considered, some steps toward the Austrian capitalisation fund have been taken, etc. Even though it is still early to anticipate the way labour courts will interpret some new regulations – as may be the case of the redundancy for economic reasons based on the new rules–,[6] there is no doubt these reforms overall try to reallocate bargaining power from workers and labour unions towards firms, and they might end up having an impact on persistence.[7] In addition, as a result of the crisis and the labour market reforms, it becomes crystal-clear that, from 2009 onwards, a significant relative adjustment in terms of wages and unit labour costs has occurred in Spain vis-à-vis other Eurozone countries.[8] All these facts lead us to wonder whether, once the crisis ends,[9] the problems of the Spanish unemployment differential and its high persistence, upon which our work seeks to shed new light, will continue to be an important issue.

References

Bande R, Fernández M, Montuenga V (2008) Regional unemployment in Spain: disparities, business cycle and wage setting. Labour Econ 15(5):885–914

Bande R, Karanassou M (2009) Labour market flexibility and regional unemployment rate dynamics: Spain 1980–1985. Pap Reg Sci 88(1):181–207

Bentolila S, Dolado JJ (1994) Labour flexibility and wages: lessons from Spain. Econo Policy 9(18):55–99

Bentolila S, Dolado JJ, Jimeno JF (2012) The "New" new labour market reform in Spain: objectives, instruments, and shortcomings. CESifo DICE Report 10(2):3–7

Bentolila S, Izquierdo M, Jimeno JF (2010) Negociación Colectiva: La Gran Reforma Pendiente. Papeles de Economía Española 124:176–192

Blanchard OJ, Jaumotte F, Loungani P (2013) Labor Market Policies and IMF Advice in Advanced Economies During the Great Recession. International Monetary Fund (IMF), Staff Discussion Note No. SDN/13/02

---

[5] For example, the 1994 labour reform brought in some mechanisms akin to those present in the most recent reforms. It should be stressed that these mechanisms were hardly brought into play in practice.

[6] In Spain it is customary that labour courts tend to favour workers regarding the interpretation of the existing rules.

[7] Another component of the 2012 labour reform is the one intended to remove the principle of "ultraactivity", which facilitates the inertia of collective agreements until another new agreement is reached. Now, under the new rules, if a new agreement is not achieved after one year, other options are explored. This issue is leading to legal confrontations since the summer of 2013.

[8] Unfortunately, mark-ups and other factors have not adjusted as much, thereby rendering the overall competitive gain moderate.

[9] The consensus among economists on the economic recovery –and on the labour market improvement– is for it to be sluggish —see for instance García-Cintado and Usabiaga (2013).

Blanchard OJ, Wolfers J (2000) The role of shocks and institutions in the rise of European unemployment: the aggregate evidence. Econo J 110(462):1–33

Calmfors L, Driffill J (1998) Bargaining structure, corporatism and macroeconomic performance. Econ Policy 3(6):14–61

Dolado JJ, Jimeno JF (1997) The causes of Spanish unemployment: a structural VAR approach. Eur Econ Rev 41(7):1281–1307

Gómez F, Usabiaga C (2001) Las Estimaciones del Desempleo de Equilibrio de la Economía Española: Una Panorámica. Revista de Economía Aplicada 9(27):103–129

Jaumotte F (2011) The Spanish Labor Market in a Cross-Country Perspective, International Monetary Fund (IMF), Working Paper No. 11/11

Jimeno JF, Bentolila S (1998) Regional unemployment persistence (Spain 1976–1994). Labour Econ 5(1):25–51

Jimeno JF, Thomas C (2011) Collective bargaining, firm heterogeneity and unemployment. Banco de España, Documento de Trabajo No. 1131

Nickell S (1997) Unemployment and labor market rigidities: Europe versus North America. J Econ Perspect 11(3):55–74

Usabiaga C (2004) *El Diferencial de Desempleo Andaluz*, Aconcagua, Sevilla

Usabiaga C (2007) "La Reforma del Mercado de Trabajo: El Caso Español", *Papeles de Economía Española*, 111, pp 177–197

Bentolila S, Jimeno JF (2006) Spanish Unemployment: The End of the Wild Ride?. In: Werding M (ed.) Structural unemployment in western Europe: reasons and remedies. MIT Press, Cambridge, pp 317–344

Chapter 5
Concluding Remarks

Abstract This chapter provides some concluding remarks to the PANIC and Granger-causality analyses conducted in the main body of this work. Some further policy implications are also drawn. The high degree of persistence found in Spanish regional unemployment calls for cautious aggregate demand stabilization policies, since they may exert permanent (or at least long-lasting) effects on Spanish unemployment. The high degree of persistence in unemployment further gives an indication that labour market reforms implemented in the Spanish economy in recent decades were not optimally designed to combat the underlying sources of hysteresis. Once the current crisis comes to an end, analysts will be able to assess the benefits reaped from the 2010–2012 labour market reforms and whether they have eroded some of the well-rooted persistence mechanisms at work in the Spanish labour market.

Keywords Spanish labour market · Conclusions

This work investigates the time series properties of the unemployment rate of the Spanish regions over the period 1976–2011. For that purpose, we employ the PANIC procedures of Bai and Ng (2004), which allows us to decompose the observed unemployment rate series into a common factor component and an idiosyncratic component. This enables us to identify the exact source behind the hysteretic behaviour found in Spanish regional unemployment. Overall, our analysis with three different proxies for the excess of labour supply renders strong support for the hysteresis hypothesis, which appears to be caused by a common stochastic trend driving all the regional unemployment rate series. The PANIC procedures have provided strong evidence that the idiosyncratic series are stationary and that a common stochastic factor appears to be the driving force behind the nonstationarity in the observed series.

An important policy implication of our result (hysteresis) is that stabilisation policy may have permanent (or at least long-lasting) effects on Spanish unemployment. In this context, the level of aggregate demand and the corresponding policies deserve great attention. Restrictive demand policies aimed at the achievement of the Maastricht criteria and the disinflation targets of central banks

A. García-Cintado et al., *Spanish Regional Unemployment*, SpringerBriefs in Economics, DOI: 10.1007/978-3-319-03686-1_5,

may have imposed a very costly burden on the Spanish economy. This has contributed to the prevailing tendency of Spanish regional unemployment rates to rise from the already high level reached after the first oil shock. In addition, this high degree of persistence in unemployment further gives an indication that labour market reforms implemented in the Spanish economy in recent decades were not optimally designed to combat the underlying sources of hysteresis. In this regard, it will take some time for economists and analysts alike to utterly assess with hindsight the effects of the 2010–2012 Spanish labour reforms, undertaken in the midst of a severe economic crisis, characterised by a lack of growth and a sharp increase in unemployment. In essence, these flexibility-enhancing labour market reforms provide firms with greater bargaining power.

In the second part of the analysis we tried to determine the macroeconomic and institutional factors that are able to explain the time series evolution of the common factor obtained, and in turn help us shed light on the ultimate sources of hysteretic behaviour in Spanish unemployment. In addition to a group of variables whose relationship with the unemployment rate proves hard to be explained straightforwardly, it is worth stating that our empirical analysis points to some of the variables highlighted by the literature as the main causes of the high and persistent Spanish unemployment (EPL, unions, unemployment benefits, minimum wage, labour cost pressure, mismatch, low productivity, insufficient ALMPs, etc.). This aforesaid literature is comprised by different theories such as "Eurosclerosis", segmented or dual labour markets (insider–outsider model), long-term unemployment predicament, union models, wage rigidity, etc. In this sense, our empirical work can be deemed to be a good supplement to previous contributions in this field; a kind of confirmatory analysis. Finally, once the current crisis comes to an end, we again advise that careful evaluations of the recent labour market reforms should be conducted, which might have eroded some of the well-rooted persistence mechanisms at work in the Spanish labour market.

Reference

Bai J, Ng S (2004) A panic attack on unit roots and cointegration. Econometrica 72(4):1127–1177

Appendix
Tables and Figures

Table A1 Data description and sources

Variable	Source
Labour productivity index (annual)	OECD (2012h)
Total factor productivity (annual, value added-based)	Timmer et al. (2007)
TFP growth (annual)	OECD (2012h)
Inflation (monthly)	National Statistical Office (2012a)
Change in inflation (monthly)	National Statistical Office (2012a)
CPI change (quarterly)	IMF (2012a)
Inflation GDP deflator (quarterly)	OECD (2012d)
Nominal money supply M1 (quarterly)	De Bustos et al. (2008)
Nominal money supply M3 (quarterly)	De Bustos et al. (2008)
Per capita real GDP (annual)	OECD (2012f)
Gross value added constant prices (annual)	De la Fuente (2009)
GDP growth (annual)	OECD (2012f)
GDP growth (annual)	World Bank (2012)
Current account balance as % of GDP (annual)	OECD (2012d)
Current account balance as % of GDP (annual)	IMF (2012b)
Trade as % of GDP (annual)	World Bank (2012)
Terms of trade adjustment (annual)	World Bank (2012)
Real interest rate (annual)	IMF (2012a)
Real interest rate (quarterly)	Own calculations based on European Central Bank (2012) and on National Statistical Office (2012a)
Real interest rate (annual)	Own calculations based on OECD (2012a) and on National Statistical Office (2012a)
Real effective exchange rate index (annual)	World Bank (2012)
Real effective exchange rate real unit labour cost index (quarterly)	IMF (2012a)
Unit labour cost index (annual)	OECD (2012d)
Real unit labour cost (quarterly)	OECD (2012d)
Unit labour cost growth	OECD (2012d)

(continued)

A. García-Cintado et al., *Spanish Regional Unemployment*, SpringerBriefs in Economics,
DOI: 10.1007/978-3-319-03686-1,

Table A1 (continued)

Variable	Source
Capital stock as % of total output (annual)	Own calculations based on De Bustos et al. (2008)
Capital stock as % of total output (annual)	Own calculations based on Boscá et al. (2007)
GFCF as % of GDP (annual)	World Bank (2012)
GFCF as % of GDP (quarterly)	De Bustos et al. (2008)
Science and Technology Expenditure as % of GDP (annual)	OECD (2012e)
Public spending as % of GDP (annual)	IMF (2012b)
Tax revenue as % of GDP (annual)	OECD (2012i)
Government Revenue as % of GDP (annual)	IMF (2012b)
Government net lending as % of GDP (annual)	OECD (2012d)
Government net lending as % of GDP (annual)	IMF (2012b)
Government Debt as % of GDP (annual)	IMF (2012b)
Housing prices (annual)	Own calculations based on FBBVA-IVIE (2009) and on National Statistical Office (2012d)
Working age population (quarterly)	National Statistical Office (2012b)
Employment rate (quarterly)	National Statistical Office (2012b)
Labour participation rate (quarterly)	National Statistical Office (2012b)
Inactivity rate (quarterly)	National Statistical Office (2012b)
Long-term unemployment as % of total unemployment (quarterly)	OECD (2012c)
Labour market tightness (vacancies/unemployment, quarterly)	Own calculations based on OECD (2012c)
Ordinary wage cost (quarterly)	National Statistical Office (2012c)
Real growth of ordinary wage cost (quarterly)	Own calculations based on National Statistical Office (2012c) and on National Statistical Office (2012a)
Total wage cost (quarterly)	Own calculations based on National Statistical Office (2012c)
Real growth of total wage cost (quarterly)	Own calculations based on National Statistical Office (2012c) and on National Statistical Office (2012a)
Hourly wages index (quarterly)	IMF (2012a)
Mean wage (annual)	FRDB-IMF (2011)
Real growth of mean wage (annual)	Own calculations based on FRDB-IMF (2011) and on National Statistical Office (2012a)
Minimum wage	FRDB-IMF (2011)
Real growth of minimum wage (annual)	Own calculations based on FRDB-IMF (2011) and on National Statistical Office (2012a)
Minimum wage as % of median wage (annual)	FRDB-IMF (2011)
Minimum wage as % of mean wage (annual)	FRDB-IMF (2011)

(continued)

Table A1 (continued)

Variable	Source
Monthly minimum wage (annual)	FRDB-IMF (2011)
Real growth of monthly minimum wage (annual)	Own calculations based on FRDB-IMF (2011) and on National Statistical Office (2012a)
Annual working hours (annual)	OECD (2012c)
Full-time workers over total (quarterly)	National Statistical Office (2012b)
Part-time Workers over total (quarterly)	National Statistical Office (2012b)
Workers under open-ended contracts over total (quarterly)	National Statistical Office (2012b)
Workers under fixed-term contracts over total (quarterly)	National Statistical Office (2012b)
Workers aged 16–24 over total (quarterly)	National Statistical Office (2012b)
Workers aged 25–54 over total (quarterly)	National Statistical Office (2012b)
Workers aged 55 and older over total (quarterly)	National Statistical Office (2012b)
Workers in agriculture over total (quarterly)	National Statistical Office (2012b)
Workers in industry over total (quarterly)	National Statistical Office (2012b)
Workers in construction over total (quarterly)	National Statistical Office (2012b)
Workers in services over total (quarterly)	National Statistical Office (2012b)
Females workers over total (quarterly)	National Statistical Office (2012b)
Males workers over total (quarterly)	National Statistical Office (2012b)
Unemployment benefits (quarterly)	De Bustos et al. (2008)
Net migration flows (annual)	De la Fuente (2009)
Oil price (US dollar) (monthly)	Federal Reserve Bank of St. Louis (2012)
Oil price (euro) (monthly)	Federal Reserve Bank of St. Louis (2012)
Energy price index (quarterly)	De Bustos et al. (2008)
Net assets as % of GDP (quarterly)	De Bustos et al. (2008)
Net international investment position	Bank of Spain (2012)
Employment protection (annual)	OECD (2012c)
People living in Urban areas (%) (annual)	World Bank (2012)
Tax wedge (%) (annual)	Own calculations based on OECD (2012f) and on OECD (2012i)
Union coverage (%) (annual)	Visser (2012)
Benefit replacement rate (annual)	OECD (2012c)
Active labour market policies (%) (annual)	OECD (2012c)
Human capital (%) (annual)	OECD (2012b)
Product markets degree of liberalization (annual)	OECD (2012g)
Total social security contributions marginal rate (annual)	OECD (2012i)
Employer social security contributions marginal rate (annual)	OECD (2012i)
Unemployment benefits gross replacement rate year 1 (annual)	FRDB-IMF (2011)
Unemployment benefits gross replacement rate year 2 (annual)	FRDB-IMF (2011)

(continued)

Table A1 (continued)

Variable	Source
Unemployment benefits gross replacement rate average over 2 years (annual)	FRDB-IMF (2011)
Unemployment benefits coverage (annual)	FRDB-IMF (2011)
Benefit duration index (annual)	Own calculations based on Nickell and Nunziata (2001)
Union density (annual)	OECD (2012c)
Union density (annual)	Visser (2012)

Table A2 Cross-sectional dependence in SPEE unemployment and job-seekers rate

	SPEE unemployment rate	Job-seekers rate	SPEE unemployment rate	Job-seekers rate
	No trend specification		Trend specification	
LM test	146.282*	132.168*	147.405*	132.843*
p-value	0.000	0.000	0.000	0.000
CD test	46.156*	43.412*	46.391*	43.545*
p-value	0.000	0.000	0.000	0.000

Note The CD-statistic and the LM-statistic test for the null of cross-sectional independence. The CD-statistic is distributed as a two-tailed standard normal distribution and the LM-statistic test as a $\chi^2_{N(N-1)/2}$ distribution. * implies rejection of the null hypothesis at the 1 % significance level

Table A3 Panel analysis of non-stationarity in idiosyncratic and common components of SPEE unemployment rate

Region	No trend specification			Trend specification			$\frac{\sigma(\Delta\hat{e}_{it})}{\sigma(\Delta y_{it})}$	$\frac{\sigma(\lambda_i'F_t)}{\sigma(\hat{e}_{it})}$
	k	$ADF_y^c(i)$	$ADF_{\hat{e}}^c(i)$	k	$ADF_y^\tau(i)$	$ADF_{\hat{e}}^\tau(i)$		
Andalusia	8	−1.635	−0.720	8	−2.058	−2.006	0.543	1.911
Aragon	7	−2.405	−2.575**	7	−2.514	−2.573*	0.638	2.626
Asturias	5	−3.045**	−3.221***	5	−3.153*	−2.693**	0.729	1.342
Balearic Islands	2	−1.783	−1.692*	2	−2.906	−2.068	0.826	1.859
Basque Country	7	−1.770	−0.870	7	−2.486	−2.525*	0.730	1.112
Canary Islands	8	−2.162	−2.178**	8	−2.191	−2.166	0.691	2.145
Cantabria	7	−2.473	−2.593***	7	−2.617	−2.450*	0.747	2.583
Castilla Leon	4	−2.523	−2.758***	4	−2.548	−2.642**	0.576	2.040
Castilla-La Mancha	6	−2.358	−1.484	6	−2.359	−2.284	0.644	2.725
Catalonia	6	−2.384	−1.891*	6	−2.768	−2.360*	0.581	1.150
Extremadura	8	−1.883	−2.096**	8	−1.956	−2.542*	0.556	1.851
Galicia	7	−2.260	−2.050**	7	−2.153	−1.634	0.766	0.769
Madrid	7	−2.684*	−2.749***	7	−2.993	−2.981**	0.678	2.015
Murcia	8	−2.177	−1.736*	8	−2.204	−1.700	0.719	2.508
Navarra	7	−1.958	−1.549	7	−2.300	−2.021	0.686	1.821
Rioja	6	−2.318	−1.690*	6	−2.306	−2.160	0.782	1.662
Valencian Community	8	−2.267	−1.686*	8	−2.442	−1.882	0.544	2.153
Critical Values								
1 %		−3.430	−2.580		−3.960	−3.167		
5 %		−2.860	−1.950		−3.410	−2.577		
10 %		−2.570	−1.620		−3.120	−2.314		
Pooled Statistics								
		$P_{\hat{e}}^c$	111.387***		$P_{\hat{e}}^\tau$	77.843***		
		$Z_{\hat{e}}^c$	9.385***		$Z_{\hat{e}}^\tau$	5.317***		

(continued)

Table A3 (continued)

Common Factor Analysis	Critical Values				Critical Values				
Statistic		1 %	5 %	10 %	Statistic		1 %	5 %	10 %
$ADF^{c}_{\hat{F}}$	−2.250	−3.430	−2.860	−2.570	$ADF^{\tau}_{\hat{F}}$	−2.395	−3.960	−3.410	−3.120

Note The augmented autoregressions employed in the ADF analysis set a maximum lag-order equal to $p = 4(T/100)^{1/4}$. $P_{\hat{e}}$ is distributed as χ^2_{34}, with 1, 5 and 10 % critical values equal to 56.061, 48.602 and 44.903, respectively. $Z_{\hat{e}}$ is distributed as N(0, 1) with 1, 5 and 10 % critical values equal to 2.326, 1.645 and 1.282. ***, ** and * imply rejection of the null hypothesis at 1, 5 and 10 %, respectively

Table A4 Panel analysis of non-stationarity in idiosyncratic and common components of SPEE job-seekers rate

Region	No trend specification			Trend specification			$\frac{\sigma(\Delta\hat{e}_{it})}{\sigma(\Delta y_{it})}$	$\frac{\sigma(\lambda_i' F_t)}{\sigma(\hat{e}_{it})}$
	k	$ADF_y^c(i)$	$ADF_{\hat{e}}^c(i)$	k	$ADF_y^\tau(i)$	$ADF_{\hat{e}}^\tau(i)$		
Andalusia	8	−2.124	−0.803	8	−2.108	−1.280	0.574	2.632
Aragon	8	−2.068	−1.955**	8	−2.088	−1.938	0.526	5.569
Asturias	6	−2.728*	−2.493**	6	−2.497	−1.953	0.645	1.754
Balearic Islands	4	−2.380	−1.840*	2	−2.272	−1.650	0.787	1.854
Basque Country	7	−1.940	−0.806	7	−2.224	−2.476*	0.718	1.807
Canary Islands	8	−2.106	−2.730***	8	−2.042	−2.850**	0.620	5.083
Cantabria	5	−2.282	−3.427***	5	−2.193	−3.805***	0.649	8.436
Castilla Leon	5	−2.217	−2.018**	5	−2.141	−2.000	0.502	2.461
Castilla-La Mancha	6	−1.998	0.547	6	−2.026	−0.719	0.593	3.813
Catalonia	5	−2.344	−1.533	5	−2.353	−1.265	0.489	1.885
Extremadura	7	−2.324	−1.802*	0	−1.966	−2.199	0.699	3.458
Galicia	8	−1.789	−1.264	8	−1.920	−1.441	0.673	1.181
Madrid	7	−2.552	−2.260**	7	−2.520	−2.829**	0.595	3.259
Murcia	8	−1.934	−1.958**	8	−1.952	−1.369	0.612	4.146
Navarra	7	−2.185	−1.584	7	−2.169	−2.075	0.676	3.037
Rioja	6	−1.920	−1.163	6	−1.941	−2.892**	0.682	4.866
Valencian Community	8	−2.184	−1.681*	8	−2.182	−1.621	0.483	3.921
Critical Values								
1 %		−3.430	−2.580		−3.960	−3.167		
5 %		−2.860	−1.950		−3.410	−2.577		
10 %		−2.570	−1.620		−3.120	−2.314		
Pooled Statistics								
		$P_{\hat{e}}^c$	94.882***		$P_{\hat{e}}^\tau$	66.624***		
		$Z_{\hat{e}}^c$	7.383***		$Z_{\hat{e}}^\tau$	3.956**		

(continued)

Table A4 (continued)

Common Factor Analysis	Critical Values				Critical Values				
Statistic		1 %	5 %	10 %	Statistic		1 %	5 %	10 %
$ADF^{c}_{\hat{F}}$	−2.265	−3.430	−2.860	−2.570	$ADF^{\tau}_{\hat{F}}$	−2.237	−3.960	−3.410	−3.120

Note The augmented autoregressions employed in the ADF analysis set a maximum lag-order equal to $p = 4(T/100)^{1/4}$. $P_{\hat{e}}$ is distributed as χ^2_{34}, with 1, 5 and 10 % critical values equal to 56.061, 48.602 and 44.903, respectively. $Z_{\hat{e}}$ is distributed as N(0, 1) with 1, 5 and 10 % critical values equal to 2.326, 1.645 and 1.282. ***, ** and * imply rejection of the null hypothesis at 1, 5 and 10 %, respectively

Table A5 Granger-causality analysis (all variables)

Variables	Granger-causality		Unit-root tests			
	Statistical significance	P-value	ADF	DF-GLS	E-R-S	Ng-Perron
Labour productivity	10 %	0.0639	I(2)	I(2)	I(2)	I(0) 10 %
TFP-GVA	No G-C	0.5396	I(2)	I(2)	I(2)	I(2)
TFP Growth	10 %	0.0805	I(1)	I(2)	I(1)	I(0) 1 %
Inflation-CPI	No G-C	0.7051	I(1)	I(2)	I(1)	I(2)
Inflation-GDPDEFL	No G-C	0.2382	I(1)	I(2)	I(2)	I(2)
CPI change	No G-C	0.9576	I(1)	I(2)	I(2)	I(2)
Housing prices	1 %	0.0005	I(2)	I(2)	I(0) 1 %	I(0) 1 %
M1	No G-C	0.8411	I(1)	I(1)	I(1)	I(1)
M3	5 %	0.0430	I(0) 1 %	I(1)	I(0) 1 %	I(1)
Per capita real GDP	1 %	0.0000	I(1)	I(0) 10 %	I(0) 5 %	I(0) 5 %
Gross value added	1 %	0.0000	I(1)	I(1)	I(1)	I(1)
GDP growth OECD	10 %	0.0746	I(1)	I(0) 1 %	I(1)	I(2)
GDP growth WDI-WB	No G-C	0.6357	I(1)	I(1)	I(1)	I(2)
Current account OECD	1 %	0.0000	I(0) 5 %	I(0) 5 %	I(0) 5 %	I(0) 5 %
Current account IMF	1 %	0.0000	I(0) 10 %	I(0) 10 %	I(0) 5 %	I(0) 5 %
Trade over GDP	10 %	0.0703	I(0) 10 %	I(1)	I(0) 1 %	I(0) 1 %
Terms of trade adjustment	No G-C	0.9930	I(0) 5 %	I(0) 5 %	I(0) 1 %	I(0) 5 %
Real interest rate IMF	No G-C	0.9317	I(0) 5 %	I(2)	I(2)	I(2)
Real interest rate ECB/CPI-NSI	No G-C	0.4541	I(1)	I(1)	I(1)	I(1)
Real interest rate OECD/CPI-NSI	No G-C	0.4564	I(1)	I(I)	I(I)	I(2)
Real effective exchange rate (REER)	No G-C	0.6637	I(0) 5 %	I(1)	I(1)	I(0) 10 %
REER-RULC	No G-C	0.9758	I(1)	I(2)	I(2)	I(2)
ULCs index	5 %	0.0126	I(2)	I(2)	I(2)	I(2)
ULCDR	No G-C	0.8330	I(0) 5 %	I(1)	I(1)	I(1)
ULC growth	1 %	0.0032	I(1)	I(2)	I(1)	I(2)

(continued)

Table A5 (continued)

Variables	Granger-causality		Unit-root tests			
	Statistical significance	P-value	ADF	DF-GLS	E-R-S	Ng-Perron
Capital stock (% GDP) BDMORES	5 %	0.0352	I(0) 5 %	I(0) 5 %	I(0) 1 %	I(0) 1 %
Capital stock (% GDP) BDREMS	5 %	0.0246	I(2)	I(2)	I(2)	I(2)
Gross fixed capital Formation (GFKF, % GDP) WDI	1 %	0.0000	I(0) 5 %	I(0) 5 %	I(0) 5 %	I(0) 5 %
GFKF (% GDP) Bdrems	1 %	0.0002	I(1)	I(1)	I(1)	I(1)
Science and technology expenditure	No G-C	0.8615	I(2)	I(1)	I(1)	I(1)
Public spending (% GDP)	1 %	0.0004	I(0) 5 %	I(1)	I(0) 5 %	I(0) 1 %
Revenue (% GDP)	10 %	0.0555	I(1)	I(1)	I(1)	I(1)
Tax revenue (% GDP)	5 %	0.0267	I(1)	I(2)	I(1)	I(2)
Government net lending OECD	1 %	0.0000	I(0) 10 %	I(1)	I(0) 5 %	I(0) 10 %
Government borrowing/lending IMF	1 %	0.0001	I(0) 5 %	I(0) 1 %	I(0) 1 %	I(0) 1 %
Government debt (% GDP)	1 %	0.0000	I(2)	I(2)	I(0) 1 %	I(0) 1%
Population over 16	No G-C	0.8977	I(0) 1%	I(0) 10%	I(0) 1%	I(0) 1%
Employment rate	1%	0.0000	I(1)	I(1)	I(1)	I(1)
Labour participation rate	No G-C	0.1075	I(1)	I(2)	I(2)	I(2)
Inactiviy rate	10 %	0.0871	I(1)	I(2)	I(2)	I(2)
Long term unemployment (% total unemployment)	No G-C	0.4898	I(1)	I(1)	I(2)	I(1)
Labour tightness (vacancies/unemployment)	1 %	0.0000	I(1)	I(1)	I(1)	I(1)
Ordinary wage cost	No G-C	0.1097	I(2)	I(1)	I(0) 10 %	I(0) 5 %
Growth rate of real ordinary wage cost	No G-C	0.5103	I(0) 1 %	I(2)	I(1)	I(2)
Total wage cost	1 %	0.0076	I(2)	I(1)	I(1)	I(1)
Growth rate of real total wage cost	No G-C	0.6620	I(0) 1 %	I(2)	I(1)	I(2)
Hourly wages index	No G-C	0.6259	I(2)	I(2)	I(2)	I(2)
Mean wage	1 %	0.0000	I(2)	I(1)	I(1)	I(0) 10 %
Growth rate of real mean wage	No G-C	0.9949	I(0) 1 %	I(2)	I(0) 5 %	I(2)

(continued)

Table A5 (continued)

Variables	Granger-causality		Unit-root tests			
	Statistical significance	P-value	ADF	DF-GLS	E-R-S	Ng-Perron
Minimum wage	No G-C	0.2044	I(2)	I(0) 10 %	I(0) 1 %	I(0) 1 %
Ratio of minimum wage to mean wage	1 %	0.0050	I(2)	I(2)	I(2)	I(2)
Annual hours	No G-C	0.6689	I(0) 1 %	I(2)	I(2)	I(2)
Full-time occupied workers over total (%)	No G-C	0.3039	I(1)	I(2)	I(1)	I(2)
Part-time occupied workers over total (%)	No G-C	0.3039	I(1)	I(2)	I(1)	I(2)
Open-ended contracts over total (%)	No G-C	0.1421	I(1)	I(2)	I(2)	I(2)
Fixed-term contracts over total (%)	No G-C	0.1421	I(1)	I(2)	I(2)	I(2)
Workers from 16 to 24 over total (%)	10 %	0.0920	I(0) 10 %	I(1)	I(1)	I(1)
Workers from 25 to 54 over total (%)	No G-C	0.6984	I(1)	I(1)	I(1)	I(0) 10 %
Workers 55 and older over total (%)	No G-C	0.1221	I(2)	I(2)	I(2)	I(0) 1 %
Workers agriculture over total (%)	5 %	0.0105	I(1)	I(2)	I(2)	I(2)
Workers construction over total (%)	1 %	0.0001	I(1)	I(2)	I(2)	I(0) 10 %
Workers industry over total (%)	No G-C	0.2277	I(1)	I(1)	I(1)	I(2)
Workers services over total (%)	1 %	0.0063	I(1)	I(1)	I(1)	I(1)
Workers females over total (%)	1 %	0.0061	I(2)	I(2)	I(2)	I(2)
Workers males over total (%)	1 %	0.0061	I(2)	I(2)	I(2)	I(2)
Unemployment benefits	No G-C	0.4532	I(1)	I(1)	I(1)	I(1)
Oil price (US$)	1 %	0.0013	I(1)	I(1)	I(1)	I(1)
Oil price (€)	5 %	0.0196	I(1)	I(1)	I(1)	I(1)
Energy price	1 %	0.0021	I(1)	I(1)	I(1)	I(2)
Net assets (% GDP)	No G-C	0.2127	I(2)	I(2)	I(2)	I(0) 10 %
Net international investment position (NIIP)	5 %	0.0336	I(2)	I(2)	I(0) 1 %	I(0) 1 %
Employment protection	1 %	0.0051	I(1)	I(1)	I(1)	I(1)
Urban (%)	5 %	0.0413	I(0) 5 %	I(1)	I(2)	I(2)

(continued)

Table A5 (continued)

Variables	Granger-causality		Unit-root tests			
	Statistical significance	P-value	ADF	DF-GLS	E-R-S	Ng-Perron
Tax wage	No G-C	0.8505	I(1)	I(1)	I(1)	I(2)
Bargaining (or Union) coverage	10 %	0.0983	I(1)	I(1)	I(1)	I(1)
Benefit replacement rates	No G-C	0.5729	I(1)	I(1)	I(1)	I(1)
Active labour market policies	1 %	0.0004	I(1)	I(1)	I(1)	I(1)
Human capital	1 %	0.0076	I(2)	I(2)	I(2)	I(2)
Energy, transport and communications regulations	No G-C	0.6812	I(2)	I(0) 5 %	I(2)	I(2)
Total social security contributions marginal rate	No G-C	0.2055	I(0) 1 %	I(1)	I(1)	I(1)
Employer social security contributions marginal rate	No G-C	0.9083	I(0) 1 %	I(1)	I(1)	I(1)
Unemployment benefits gross replacement rate average over 2 years	1 %	0.0022	I(0) 1 %	I(1)	I(1)	I(1)
Unemployment benefits coverage	No G-C	0.1563	I(1)	I(1)	I(1)	I(1)
Benefit duration index	1 %	0.0005	I(0) 5 %	I(1)	I(2)	I(2)
Union density (Interpol) OECD	No G-C	0.1005	I(1)	I(1)	I(1)	I(1)
Union density Visser	No G-C	0.8523	I(0) 10 %	I(0) 5 %	I(2)	I(2)

Note In those cases in which the unit root null hypothesis is rejected at conventional significance levels, the significance level is shown in the respective cells

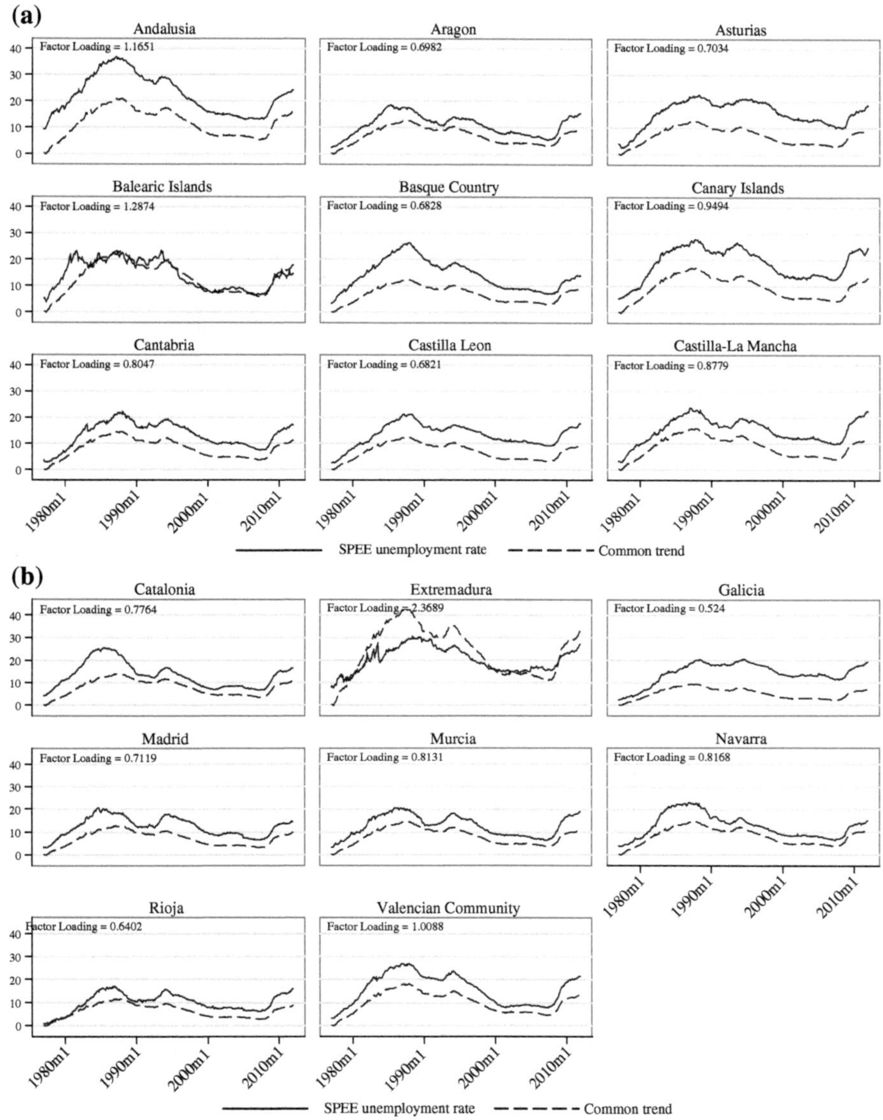

Fig. A1 **a** Regional SPEE unemployment rates and the common trend. **b** Regional SPEE unemployment rates and the common trend

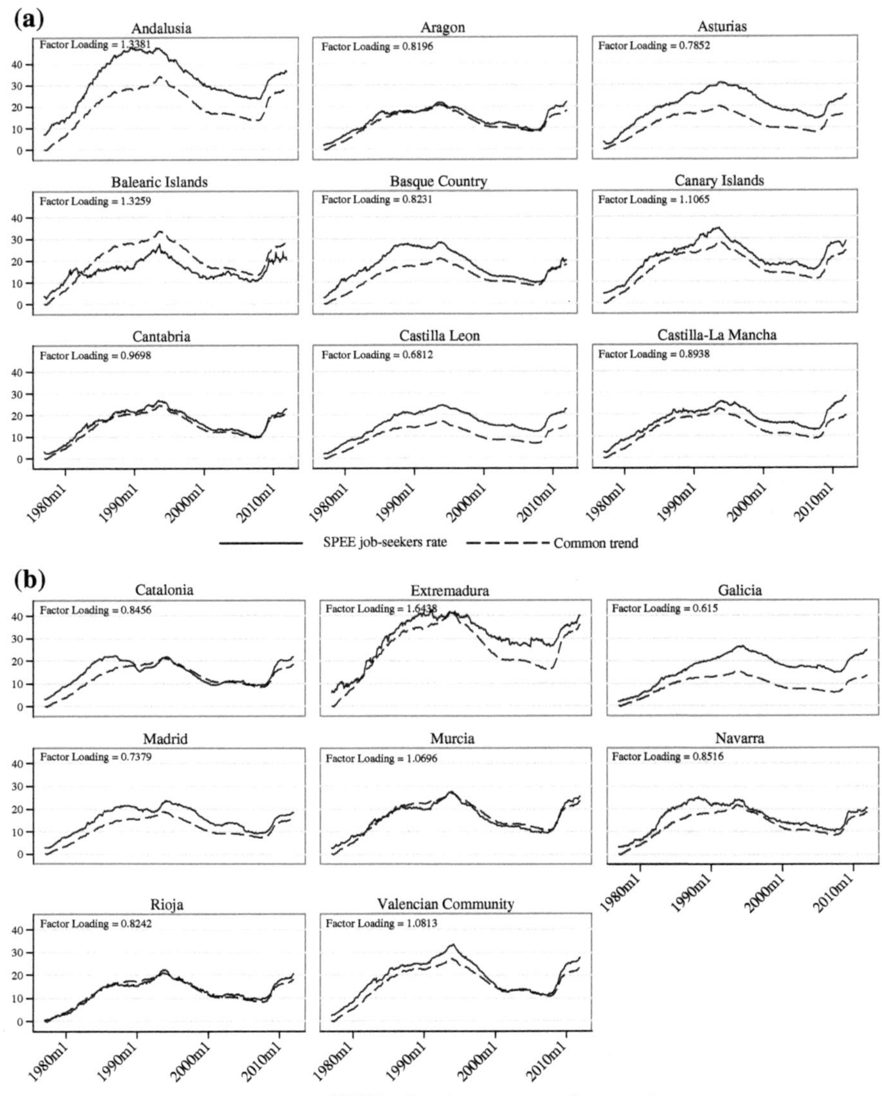

Fig. A2 **a** Regional SPEE job-seekers rates and the common trend. **b** Regional SPEE job-seekers rates and the common trend

References

Anelli M, Catania A, Basso G, Colussi T, Monti P, Zhelyazkova M, Eichhorst W (2012) FRDB-IZA database. Fondazione Rodolfo Debenedetti and Institute for the Study of Labour, Bonn

Bank of Spain (2012) Economic indicators. Bank of Spain, Madrid

Boscá JE, Bustos A, Díaz A, Doménech R, Ferri J, Pérez E, Puch L (2007) The REMSDB macroeconomic database of the Spanish economy. Ministerio de Hacienda y Administraciones Públicas (D-2007-03), Madrid

De Bustos A, Cutanda A, Díaz A, Escribá FJ, Murgui MJ, Sanz MJ (2008) La BD.MORES en base 2000: nuevas estimaciones y variables. Dirección General de Presupuestos, Ministerio de Economía y Hacienda (D-2008-02), Madrid

De la Fuente A (2009) Series Enlazadas de algunos agregados económicos nacionales y regionales, 1955–2007, Versión 2.1, mimeo. Instituto de Análisis Económico (CSIC), Barcelona

European Central Bank (2012) Monetary and financial statistics. European Central Bank, Frankfurt

FBBVA-IVIE (2009) Spanish capital stock in housing and its territorial distribution (1990–2007). BBVA Foundation and Valencian Economic Research Institute, Valencia

Federal Reserve Bank of St. Louis (2012) Federal reserve economic data (FRED). Federal Reserve Bank of St. Louis, St. Louis

FRDB-IMF (2011) FRDB-IMF labour institutions database (1980–2005). Fondazione Rodolfo Debenedetti and International Monetary Fund, Milan

IMF (2012a) International financial statistics. International Monetary Fund, Washington

IMF (2012b) World economic outlook database. International Monetary Fund, Washington

National Statistical Office (2012a) Consumer price index. National Statistical Office, Madrid

National Statistical Office (2012b) Labour force survey. National Statistical Office, Madrid

National Statistical Office (2012c) Quarterly labour cost survey. National Statistical Office, Madrid

National Statistical Office (2012d) Housing price index. National Statistical Office, Madrid

Nickell W (2006) The CEP-OECD institutions data set (1960–2004). Centre for Economic Performance (CEP), London School of Economics and Political Science, London

Nickell S, Nunziata L (2001) Labour market institutions database. Centre for Economic Performance (CEP), London School of Economics and Political Science, London

OECD (2012a) OECD economic outlook, 91. Organisation for Economic Cooperation and Development, Paris

OECD (2012b) OECD education statistics. Organisation for Economic Cooperation and Development, Paris

OECD (2012c) OECD employment and labour market statistics. Organisation for Economic Cooperation and Development, Paris

OECD (2012d) OECD main economic indicators. Organisation for Economic Cooperation and Development, Paris

OECD (2012e) OECD main science and technology indicators. Organisation for Economic Cooperation and Development, Paris

OECD (2012f) OECD national accounts. Organisation for Economic Cooperation and Development, Paris

OECD (2012g) OECD product market regulation statistics. Organisation for Economic Cooperation and Development, Paris

OECD (2012h) OECD productivity statistics. Organisation for Economic Cooperation and Development, Paris

OECD (2012i) OECD tax statistics. Organisation for Economic Cooperation and Development, Paris

Timmer MP, O'Mahony M, van Ark B (2007) EU KLEMS growth and productivity accounts: an overview. Groningen Growth and Development Centre, Groningen

Visser J (2012) Wage setting, State intervention and social pacts in 34 countries between 1960 and 2007. Amsterdam Institute for Advanced Labour Studies (AIAS), University of Amsterdam, Amsterdam

World Bank (2012) World development indicators 2012 database. World Bank, Washington

MIX
Papier aus verantwortungsvollen Quellen
Paper from responsible sources
FSC® C105338
www.fsc.org

If you have any concerns about our products,
you can contact us on
ProductSafety@springernature.com

In case Publisher is established outside the EU,
the EU authorized representative is:
Springer Nature Customer Service Center GmbH
Europaplatz 3, 69115 Heidelberg, Germany

Printed by Libri Plureos GmbH
in Hamburg, Germany